Being Best Man
FOR DUMMIES

A Wiley Brand

2ND EDITION

by Dominic Bliss

FOR DUMMIES

A Wiley Brand

Being the Best Man For Dummies®, 2nd Edition

Published by: **John Wiley & Sons, Ltd.,** The Atrium, Southern Gate, Chichester, www.wiley.com

This edition first published 2013

© 2013 John Wiley & Sons, Ltd, Chichester, West Sussex.

Registered office

John Wiley & Sons Ltd, The Atrium, Southern Gate, Chichester, West Sussex, PO19 8SQ, United Kingdom

For details of our global editorial offices, for customer services and for information about how to apply for permission to reuse the copyright material in this book please see our website at www.wiley.com.

Wiley publishes in a variety of print and electronic formats and by print-on-demand. Some material included with standard print versions of this book may not be included in e-books or in print-on-demand. If this book refers to media such as a CD or DVD that is not included in the version you purchased, you may download this material at http://booksupport.wiley.com. For more information about Wiley products, visit www.wiley.com.

Designations used by companies to distinguish their products are often claimed as trademarks. All brand names and product names used in this book are trade names, service marks, trademarks or registered trademarks of their respective owners. The publisher is not associated with any product or vendor mentioned in this book.

For general information on our other products and services, please contact our Customer Care Department within the U.S. at 877-762-2974, outside the U.S. at (001) 317-572-3993, or fax 317-572-4002. For technical support, please visit www.wiley.com/techsupport.

For technical support, please visit www.wiley.com/techsupport.

A catalogue record for this book is available from the British Library.

ISBN 978-1-118-65043-1 (hardback/paperback); ISBN 978-1-118-65042-4 (eMobi); ISBN 978-1-118-65038-7 (ePDF); ISBN 978-1-118-65040-0 (ePub)

Printed in Great Britain by TJ International

10 9 8 7 6 5 4 3 2 1

Contents at a Glance

Table of Contents

Introduction

● ●

*I*n a previous existence, I was launch editor and feature writer for a men's wedding magazine called *Stag & Groom*. Among the articles we published, we had loads of no-nonsense advice on stag parties, speech content and wedding suits. Inevitably, whenever friends or colleagues got engaged or appointed best man, the first person they would call for advice was me. Every springtime, just as the wedding season was starting to hot up, I used to get at least a couple such calls a week, and the two topics they would be panicking about most were the stag party and the speech.

Those are the two topics I've allocated the most space to in this book. There are loads of other duties a best man needs to consider – and they're all covered in detail as well – but the stag do and the speech are the most important. They are the bench marks on which all best men are ultimately judged. Wear the wrong wedding suit, and you'll be forgiven. Forget to don your button-hole or do up your flies, and the chances are no one will notice except the bride. But mess up the stag do or the speech, and you'll be remembered for all time as the best man who got it wrong.

This book will make sure you get them right.

About This Book

I can safely say I've been to more weddings in my life than I've had birthdays. Over the last few years, in particular, as I've waved reluctantly goodbye to my 30s, I've found myself dusting down my morning suit all too regularly.

As a result, I've sat through more best man's speeches than I care to remember. Some have been witty, some have been dull, some have been cheesy and some have been hilarious. One thing a lot of them have shared, though, is an opening line that goes a bit like this: 'Being appointed best man is a bit like being asked to make love to the Queen. It's an honour, but it's something you'd really rather not do!'

Now therein lies the problem. Being best man really *is* an honour. But, when it comes down to it, it's an honour that nearly all of us would rather not have. That's where this book comes in. Throughout I've tried to beef up the honour bit and play down the scary stuff. I've boiled down the many best man's duties to their basics, stripped away the complicated, confusing bits and revealed them for what they really are – simple, practical duties that are easy to fulfil.

What You're Not to Read

As you dip in and out of this book (it's not written to be read in one sitting), you'll notice quite a few tips, warnings and things to remember. If you like, you can get away without reading a single one of them. It won't actually make you any less a best best man.

What I advise, however, is that you occasionally flick through the book and home in on those sections. They offer little nuggets of advice that will sit at the back of your mind and put you in good stead as you embark on your duties.

The blocked out sidebars are similar. Although they're not critical to the text or to your understanding of your duties, they provide interesting little asides.

Foolish Assumptions

Forgive me, but to make things a lot easier I've made a few assumptions about you, the reader. I'm assuming that you

- ✔ **Are male.** Granted, nowadays you do very occasionally get female best men. But few of them buy books advising them on their duties. If you're the exception, then I'm sorry, but you'll have to get used to all the male pronouns.

- ✔ **Like a drink.** Stag dos and weddings tend to be well lubricated. Grooms know this. Best men know this. And a groom is unlikely to appoint a best man who's not willing to play along. Even just a little bit.

✔ **Are going to be best man at a church or a registry office.** In our multiracial society, people get married under many religions and beliefs, but to keep things simple, I've referred to Church of England or civil wedding conventions throughout.

How This Book Is Organized

The book is split up into four stand-alone parts. It's entirely up to you which order you read them in. The first three parts cover the three main duties you're involved in: the stag do, the wedding ceremony and the speech. The fourth part then includes all the listy stuff that will get you thinking about the finer details of your job.

Part 1: Getting Started with Being the Best Man

Here you find out about all the diplomatic skills you're going to need in the months before the wedding: how to deal with the bride, her family and, most importantly, your groom – the man who appointed you. Then you'll be offered all the very best advice on how to organise and execute the stag do and give the groom a proper send-off he'll never forget. Or never remember, as the case may be.

Part II: Wedding Preparations and the Big Day

Your prenuptial duties are a cinch compared to the bride and groom's, but there are still lots of key things you mustn't forget. Don't worry – they're all in here. As are all your duties on the morning of the wedding and during the actual ceremony and the reception afterwards.

Part III: The Speech

The best man's speech can be a beast if you don't approach it properly. This section has all the advice you need to tame that beast. By the time the reception comes round, it'll be eating out of your hand. Hopefully, so will your audience.

Part IV: The Part of Tens

Do you need some instant ideas on where to go on the stag do? Or what activities to get everyone involved in? Look no further than The Part of Tens.

Icons Used in This Book

Stag parties and wedding days are all about planning ahead and then thinking on your feet when those plans go awry. Often, it's simply a case of damage limitation. To help you with this, I've scattered lots of icons at key stages throughout the book.

Soon after being appointed best man, you'll be glad of any advice offered to you. These little nuggets provide the most useful bits of advice.

There are so many things to remember when you're part of the wedding party. Add to this your duties as stag party organiser, and you can see why some best men crack under the pressure. These little icons serve as mini checklists or mental sticky notes.

The entire marriage process is a diplomatic minefield. What with the bride, the groom, their parents, the vicar, the chief bridesmaid, the ushers and all the stags to keep happy, you'll need some help to steer yourself clear of the mines.

Where to Go from Here

A best man's duties can vary as much as different brides' tastes in napkin colours. Some are required to organise everything from stag do to suits to speeches, right down to the finest details. Others get away pretty much scot free.

You know what your groom and his bride expect of you. And you will have certain key areas you are most worried about. If you've only got three weeks until the stag do, then jump straight in at Chapter 2. If you're sweating over the speech already, then skip to Chapter 8. Or if you need a little overview of what your general duties are, then it's Chapter 1 you need.

Part I
Getting Started with Being the Best Man

In this part . . .

- ✔ Know your key roles as best man.

- ✔ Gain all the personal and organisational skills you're going to need in the months before the wedding.

- ✔ Discover how to be cool and organised under pressure.

- ✔ Organize and execute the stag do so that it's one for the history books.

- ✔ Give the groom a proper send-off to his bachelor days he'll never forget.

Chapter 1

Best Man Basics

In This Chapter

▶ Understanding the best man's role in the wedding build-up

▶ Knowing what to do on the wedding day

▶ Grasping the qualities of a best man

*E*very member of the wedding party has a precise and well-defined role. The groom's job is to turn up on time and behave like a saint all day. The bride smiles, looks gorgeous and keeps one eye on the reception. The minister or registrar directs the ceremony. The ushers get everyone seated and organise the car parking. The bridesmaids fuss about the bride's dress. The bride's father worries about how much everything's cost him. And the bride's mother cries like a baby.

Interconnecting these roles in order to keep everyone happy and everything running smoothly is the linchpin of the wedding party. Yes, that's you, the best man. But don't worry: I'm here to help.

I'm the Best Man! What Am I Supposed to Do?

Your role as best man is a multifaceted one. You have to get the groom to the ceremony on time. You have to ensure that the guests are seated correctly and make the journey to the reception. At the reception, your speech is the one that everyone's waiting to hear. And as well as the bride and groom, how you perform on the big day is what everyone remembers after the wedding.

As best man, your *key* roles are these:

- ✔ **Organising the groom's stag do.** You can find plenty more details on how to have fun in Chapters 2 and 3.

- ✔ **Getting the groom to the ceremony.** Read Chapter 5 before kicking him out of bed on the big day.

- ✔ **Witnessing the wedding.** Finest pen and best handwriting at the ready, all is revealed in Chapter 6.

- ✔ **Organising people for the wedding photographs.** Get an idea of who's in the big picture by heading to Chapter 6.

- ✔ **Helping guests to the reception.** Help yourself to help the guests by reading Chapter 7.

- ✔ **Making a speech at the reception.** Find out what to say and what not to say by studying Chapters 8 and 9.

Fret not! You're not expected to do everything. Sure, you've got to plan ahead, be prepared, keep lists, run a tight ship and think on your feet. But lots of eager people are available to whom you can delegate tasks. The ushers are there to be at your beck and call, and you find that plenty of other guests are willing to lend a hand.

A wedding's like a supertanker. Making a slight alteration in course takes days. As long as you're aware of this and plan everything well in advance, you'll stay clear of the rocks.

Some weddings are well organised, and some are chaotic. As best man, you want to pray for the former but accept that you may get the latter. Whatever happens, keep your diary organised. With military planning and teamwork, being the best man can run smoothly. I've included a handy checklist of what to do and when to do it, as shown in Figure 1-1.

Best Man's Countdown

12 months to go
* the groom appoints you as best man
* block out the whole week before the wedding in your diary

9 months to go
* engagement party (see Chapter 1)

5 months to go
* help the groom choose his ushers (see Chapters 1 and 4)
* begin organizing the stag do (see Chapter 2)

3 months to go
* review the wedding plans with the bride and groom (see Chapter 1)
* accompany the groom to get fitted for your suits (see Chapter 4)
* start writing your speech (see Chapter 8)

2 months to go
* finalise the plans for the stag do (see Chapter 2)
* buy your present for the bride and groom
* keep practising your speech (see Chapters 8 and 9)

1 month to go
* the stag do (see Chapter 3)

2 weeks to go
* make the ushers aware of their duties (see Chapter 4)
* check the groom has bought the ring
* finalise your speech (see Chapters 8 and 9)

1 week to go
* wedding rehearsal (see Chapter 4)
* finalise the wedding schedule with the groom and print it out (see Chapter 4)
* hire the wedding suits (see Chapter 5)
* buy confetti and decorations for the wedding car (see Chapter 6)

1 day to go
* the last supper (see Chapter 5)
* charge up your mobile phone
* stuff your wallet with cash
* ask the bride and groom for messages from absent friends (see Chapter 8)
* check the groom has the ring in a safe place (see Chapter 6)

Figure 1-1: The best man's countdown to the wedding day.

The first of the best

Don't panic – best men have been around for centuries. Some historians believe that the role developed during the latter days of the Roman Empire. Back then, when the local village had run out of eligible girls, young Goths (black eyeliner, pointy shoes and all) were forced to raid neighbouring villages in search of a bride. Not the most romantic way of proposing to your future wife, eh? When the fathers and brothers realised what was going on, they did their utmost to protect the honour of their daughters and sisters, even if it meant a full-on Gothic brawl.

This period is where the best man came in. His job was to help the potential groom wrestle his chosen bride away from the family. He'd then act as henchman right up until the wedding ceremony, when he'd stand guard at the altar just in case the bride's family staged a last-minute rescue attempt.

Fortunately, nowadays, most brides have given their consent. You'd hope that their fathers were in agreement, too. The modern best man's role is now more about organisation and moral support than pure physical force.

Important Advice to Heed

The best man receives advice from all corners, some of which is good, some of which is bad. This book gives you plenty of great advice, but before you go any further, I've pulled together some basic tips to bear in mind right from the start.

Acting as the middle man

Getting married is a stressful business. Second only to moving house (oh . . . and divorce), this occasion puts more pressure on the bride and groom than most of the trials and tribulations they're likely to face during their life together – which is why you need to be tactful at all times.

Think of the bride and groom as two neighbouring countries who've just signed a peace treaty. As the diplomat chosen for the tricky job of liaising between the two, you have to be tactful. Although your loyalty ultimately lies with the groom, you must be able to support both halves of the marital divide.

Start off by reassuring the groom that you are the best, best man he could possibly have chosen. He wants to know that you're definitely not the sort to mess things up. You've taken on a tricky task. First of all, you're expected to host the stag party to end all stag parties (party on down to Chapters 2 and 3 for some help on sorting this). Then a few weeks later, you've got to don a penguin suit (check out Chapter 4 for all your sartorial needs), charm the socks off all the relatives and regale dozens of guests with a scintillating speech. (Read more on speeches in Chapters 8 and 9.)

You may be shaking like a leaf at the prospect of all of this responsibility. But don't let the groom know. He wants his right-hand man to be as cool as a cucumber.

So does the bride. She wants to pretend that the stag party isn't really going to happen. (So when you do mention the event, play down the rowdy elements.) And on the big day she wants everything to run as smoothly as the silk tie around your neck. Reassure her that this is the case – if you don't, she may tighten that tie rather uncomfortably.

Arrange a meeting with the bride and groom soon after the engagement. Offer your services in any way you can. You may find that the bride has some very solid ideas about how she wants the ceremony and reception to pan out. Before you get together, read Chapters 4 and 5 to gain a better understanding of what you may be asked to do and what a sample wedding schedule looks like. Your job isn't to stick your oar in at this juncture – what the bride says, goes.

Where you can help is with the inevitable disputes between future husband and wife. Minister or registrar, marriage and reception venues, caterers, florist, parents-in-law, pageboys, photographer, table plans – just some of the areas where the nuptial harmony gets ruffled . . . totally wrecked even. Your job is to reinstate that harmony, even if that means you making suggestions on what colour the napkins should be.

Apart from driving the groom to the wedding venue and help- ing the photographer to get people together for the group shots after the ceremony(covered in Chapters 5 and 6), the bride is in charge of virtually every other wedding detail. In meetings with the bride and groom, don't contradict the former or take sides with the latter. Bride is always right –

from little details like ushers' buttonholes, all the way up to the big things like who does the catering.

Keeping in with the in-laws

As far as the bride's parents are concerned, you're a bad influence on their daughter's chosen husband. You're the irresponsible young tyke who takes him out drinking until dawn, gets him into scrapes and generally keeps him off the straight and narrow.

At the first possible chance, you need to reverse this image that the bride's parents have of you. They're probably both going to be present at the engagement party, but if you don't already know the bride's parents, ask the bride and groom to arrange a meeting beforehand. At the very least, call them on the phone. They want to know that you're responsible and that your side of the wedding duties is in safe hands. Ease their troubled minds, especially the father of the bride. He could well be pumping his life savings into this wedding, and he doesn't want you mucking up the seating plan or delivering a crass speech.

Things get complicated when the bride's parents are divorced. All sorts of familial politics come into play, and if you're not careful, you could ruffle a few feathers. Take your lead from the bride. Dad may well be paying, but Mum wants her say, too – even if she and Dad no longer see eye to eye.

Shining at the engagement party

This celebration is your first chance to meet all the key players in the wedding. Use the engagement party as an opportunity to show both families that you really are the man for the job. Introduce yourself to those outside the immediate family. And make a mental note of the dynamics between all the different characters. Are you aware of a potential clash of personalities between the two mothers? Does the bridesmaid drink too much? Is Auntie Ethel really mad or just eccentric?

Even this early on in the marriage process, people look to you for some sort of guidance. Your job has officially started, and you're already somewhat on parade. So turn up on time, dress smartly and don't, whatever you do, drink the bar dry. If you misbehave at the engagement party, then who knows what you're going to get up to at the reception?

Being the best, best man a man can get

The clue is in your title. *Best* man. Not mediocre man. Not quite good man. But *best* man. That means all the qualities you require must be honed more finely than anyone else's.

Presumably, if you were totally unreliable, then the groom wouldn't have appointed you as bestie. Saying that, you can brush up on the qualities you need in a number of ways.

Married or single?

So what happens if the groom doesn't turn up? Are you, as best man, expected to step into his shoes and marry the bride yourself? In centuries past, that was the tradition, which was why bestie had to be a bachelor. Fortunately (or unfortunately, depending on how keen you are on the bride), that requirement is no longer applicable. If the groom jilts the bride at the altar, you may well get the blame. But you won't be obliged to take over. (For more advice on dealing with the disaster to end all wedding disasters, flick through, if you dare, to Chapter 6.)

This fact means that your marital status is irrelevant. In truth, married best men are often more competent than unmarried ones, by dint of the simple fact that they've already been through the whole rigmarole themselves. They know full well what the groom's got in store. But if you're still single, you can be an equally good best man, so you don't need to start dating just for the job.

Being responsible and tactful

Even during the wildest moments of the stag party, you should have a little voice at the back of your mind reminding you that the buck stops firmly with you. The groom is expected to act like a fool during his stag celebrations and then wander down the aisle in a blissful daze, before trotting out a three-minute speech, but you, my friend, have a lot more on your plate. You have to be responsible – yes, even at three o'clock in the morning in a nightclub. You have to be tactful – especially when the content of your speech is concerned. And you have to maintain this responsibility and tact even if things start to go awry.

Talking and listening

The best man's role starts off very much as a listening one. Listen to the bride as she frets about the table seating plan. Listen to the groom as he cries on your shoulder just days before the wedding. Listen to the registrar as he fumbles his lines at the wedding rehearsal.

Then, very quickly, your job turns into a talking role: talking loudly into the groom's ear when he oversleeps on the big day; barking instructions at the ushers; herding the guests from the ceremony to the reception; and then, delivering a rousing speech.

Communication may come naturally to you. If you're not a natural, then developing this skill is something you must work on, especially when it comes to the speech. No one's expecting a Churchillian oration or a West End-quality stand-up comedy show. Yes, your audience wants to have a laugh and be aroused emotionally. But at the same time, they all know that you're the groom's mate – not a professional speaker. With a bit of practice, most people can get by. Chapters 8 and 9 give some hints and tips on dealing with this big occasion. You may also like to seek out Kate Burton and Brinley Platts's *Building Confidence For Dummies* and Romilla Ready and Kate Burton's *Neuro-linguistic Programming For Dummies* (both published by Wiley).

Being presentable and punctual

You can't avoid the fact. You're going to have to wear a suit. You also have to wash, shave and get your hair cut. Under the spotlight at the ceremony and the reception, you're expected to look your best. So make an effort. And err on the safe side: A mullet haircut and an earring may look great at your local pub, but 20 years down the line, those wedding photos will come back to haunt you.

Make sure that you get the groom to the ceremony on time (Chapter 5 points you in the right direction). Timekeeping is your responsibility. At the engagement party, at the stag party, and on the big day, punctuality is crucial. Your groom has got enough on his mind, what with the emotional stress of getting hitched, so make sure that he's on time.

Chapter 2

Stag Do's and Stag Don'ts

*S*tag dos have moved on radically from the days of a simple curry and a booze-up. Now that men are marrying later in life, they've often got more cash to fritter away on stag celebrations. Couple that with the recent revolution in budget short-haul European air travel, and you can see why more and more husbands-to-be are opting for a whole weekend of revelry, far away from the confines of their home town (and the watchful eye of their future bride).

Of course, more money and more destinations mean a whole lot more to decide on. Best men may find themselves with flights and hotels to book, nightclubs to forewarn, activities to organise and 20 rowdy stags to marshal around a foreign city. This chapter helps you choose who to invite (see 'Guest List Only'), where to go (see 'Home or Away?'), and what to do (see 'Getting Out and About').

Guest List Only

Believe it or not, choosing who to invite on the stag do is not a simple case of jotting down a list of the groom's best friends. Mad Dog Malone will have nothing in common with that quiet bloke who works in IT. And shouldn't the bride's brother come along, too?

Stags and stagettes

Occasionally, just occasionally, you may find that your groom opts for a mixed-sex stag celebration. Or the groom and his bride agree to unite all the stags and hens for one evening during the weekend. After all, we are living in the 21st century.

This arrangement can alter proceedings somewhat – female stags may not want a five-a-side football tournament by day and a strip club at night. But plenty of daytime and evening activities can be found that appeal to both sexes. How about a day of track motor racing or go-karting followed by a top-notch evening meal and a rock concert? Neither the stag nor the stagette will turn their nose up at that.

But let's face facts. Mixed-sex stag parties are a rarity. And so they should be. The whole idea is for the groom to spend time bonding with his male friends – he can wait until the wedding to celebrate with his female friends.

The stag do guest list is like the recipe for a big seafood pie. Get the ingredients just slightly off, and you may have to call in the health inspectors. The following tips can keep you on the right track.

Clique is weak

The main purpose of the stag do, besides helping the groom wave goodbye to his bachelor days in style, is to unite the groom and all his best friends. Cliques are not welcome here. Whatever you do, try to keep everyone together in one big group.

This strategy is tricky when you've got old friends from home, mates from university, work colleagues and a future brother-in-law. Every stag do has a wildcard – that's half the fun – but as far as possible you want to limit the number of guests who you know won't make an effort to get along with everyone else. Remind the groom that he wants team players, not lone wolves.

Show me the money

Good stag dos are not cheap, and cheap stag dos are, on the whole, very bad indeed. Thanks to the dozens of budget airlines plying their trade on the Internet, a weekend abroad is much cheaper than it once was. But you can still expect to fork out up to £1,000 on a three-day break in Barcelona. Even a night in Blackpool can set you back a few hundred sheets. Here are some examples of what stag dos can cost each person:

- ✔ **Long weekend in Barcelona:** Flight £120; two hotel nights £200; food and drink £300; two days of water sports £80; football match at FC Barcelona £70; three nightclub entries £90; taxis £40. Total: £900 per person.

- ✔ **Two days in Prague:** Flight £120; two hotel nights £160; food and drink £150; two days of extreme military training £100; football match at Sparta Prague £20; two nightclub entries £20; taxis £20. Total: £590 per person.

- ✔ **Weekend in Blackpool:** Train fare £50; two hotel nights £100; food and drink £200; a day in the amusement park £50; a day of go-karting and paintballing £50; two nightclub entries £40; taxis £20. Total: £510 per person.

- ✔ **An evening in the groom's home town:** Food and drink £80; taxis £20. Total: £100 per person.

Do not invite someone who can't keep up with the pace financially as their predicament can break up the team, embarrass the groom and humiliate the bloke in question. Warn everyone in advance how much the event is going to cost them and give people the option to duck out. (I explain how to do this in 'Organising the finances', later in this chapter.)

But what if the groom has friends on radically different incomes? Although the groom's old school buddy who's now a corporate trader may not even blink at the prospect of forking out a cool grand on a long weekend in Amsterdam, his less well-paid friends may struggle just to cover a night out in Brighton.

You can get around this problem in several ways. Some grooms opt for a two-part stag do, where their more skint friends join everyone for the evening celebrations and miss out on the expensive daytime activities. Others organise two separate stag celebrations – one for their well-off friends and one for the skint people.

A friend of mine who works in The City managed to pull this off quite diplomatically. He and all his workmates were on pant-wettingly huge salaries, but most of his friends from home were on modest incomes and struggling to pay their mortgages. So, rather cleverly, he invited all the City boys on an obscenely expensive weekend to the south of France, and a week later he had a pub crawl in London for his old friends from school. Both celebrations were just as enjoyable, and nobody felt like they missed out. Most importantly, everyone could afford to be there.

The problem is that two stag parties can add to your already mounting logistical headaches – and the idea is hardly team-building. Spare a thought for my wife, who had three hen parties: one for her work friends, one for her pregnant friends who were off the alcohol and one for the party animals.

Nearest and dearest

For some reason, a tradition used to be to invite the groom's father and – get this – the bride's father. Stop! Don't even think about inviting them! In some circumstances, you may just get away with inviting the former – provided he's broad-minded and knows all his son's mates. But never in a million years should you invite the latter – a recipe for disaster. Unless, of course, the groom is marrying Kelly Osbourne, in which case Daddy can be counted on to liven up proceedings.

Inviting the bride's brother presents a trickier situation. Diplomacy suggests that he should come along. After all, you ought to have at least one representative from the bride's side of the family. But he needs to be discreet, and you need to gauge how to stop him dropping his future brother-in-law right in it.

Home or Away?

Come on. Blackpool is so passé. If the budget allows, live a little. Why not persuade the groom to really push the boat and go a bit further afield? Great stag destinations within the UK abound – surfing in Newquay, yomping in the Highlands, powerboating off the south coast. . . . But for a real adventure, what about making the most of those budget airlines and all heading off to Eastern Europe?

Before you choose between Blighty and abroad, bear in mind some crucial factors. Will work and family commitments allow the stags to take a long weekend? Don't arrange to fly out to Bangkok on a Friday night if you have to be back in London by Sunday lunchtime.

Can the groom's friends afford to fork out on foreign travel and hotel rooms? Tallinn, on the Baltic coast, is lovely in April – but not if you're freezing your bits off in a campsite.

If both time and money are tight, this doesn't mean that the stag do has to be humdrum. We live on a small but motley island. With a bit of imagination, you can stay in Britain and keep prices down but still inject some adrenalin into the weekend.

Saying that, going away for a weekend abroad is a great leveller, a fantastic ice-breaker and the perfect way to get all the stags bonding. Away from Blighty, Brits take on a different attitude. Faced with an alien language and an unfamiliar culture, they rally together. British boys also know that on foreign soil, no one will recognise them – so rowdy behaviour, the crucial ingredient of any good stag do, is guaranteed.

Choosing the Organiser

If possible, you really ought to add the personal touch and organise the stag do yourself. This fact is, after all, one of the main reasons that the groom press-ganged you into being best man. Saying that, you simply may not have the time for all the research, phone calls and paperwork required to organise a great stag party.

Do it yourself

Something of a balancing act is needed for organising the stag do. You want to take a personal responsibility in making sure that everything is just right for your groom, but at the same time, you don't want to bite off more than you can chew and end up messing up some of the key ingredients.

Reserving a table in a restaurant or ten rooms in a hotel is easy enough and hardly time-consuming, and if you make the arrangements yourself, you can make sure that everything's to the groom's personal taste. But booking everyone on to a military training course in deepest, darkest Estonia requires a lot of local knowledge. Are you sure that you want to pay a hefty credit-card deposit to a bunch of ex-soldiers via a dodgy-looking website? This kind of situation is where you're better off paying a small commission to a professional stag organiser.

Let the pros take over

If you're short of ideas or worried about logistics and organisational headaches, you can always approach one of the dozens of specialist stag companies operating in Britain (I give a long list later on). Some of these companies are very small outfits – sometimes even just one-man bands – but others employ deskloads of knowledgeable staff. The former add a small fee to cover their costs, while the latter mark up everything from travel and accommodation to activities and evening entertainment. When you've discussed your stag requirements with them over the phone, you'll soon get an idea of what kind of operation they are.

Think carefully before dismissing the idea of employing a stag company. Yes, using this service can cost substantially more than booking the hotel/travel/activities direct. But have you really got the time to phone around various companies yourself? You can save yourself a lot of hassle if you pay someone else to do the arrangements.

Besides, the overall bill is going to be split between all the stags anyway (see Chapter 3 for more on this). These companies have hundreds of contacts in the industry and are able to customise your trip to perfection.

The following companies are UK-based specialists in organising stag days and stag weekends:

- ✔ **The Barcelona Adventure Company:** www.barcelona adventure.com; 0871-711-5068

- ✔ **Bespoke Weekends:** www.bespokeweekends.co.uk; 0131 476 2474

- ✔ **Chillisauce:** www.chillisauce.co.uk; 020 7299 1831

- ✔ **Design Adventure:** www.designaventure.co.uk; 01432 830880

- ✔ **Eclipse Leisure:** www.eclipseleisure.co.uk; 01273 872230

- ✔ **Edinburgh Stag & Hen Weekends:** www.edinburgh stagandhen.co.uk; 0131 450 7113

- ✔ **Escape:** www.escapetrips.co.uk; 0117 9277173

- ✔ **Freedom:** www.freedomltd.com; 01992 655580

- ✔ **Garlands Off Road and Corporate Leisure:** www.garlandsleisure.co.uk; 01827-722123

- ✔ **Hen & Stag World:** www.henandstagworld.co.uk; 0191 206 4027

- ✔ **Ice Cube Party Weekends:** www.ice-cube.co.uk; 01943 872415

- ✔ **justplanetevents:** www.justplanetevents.com; 0845-222-3502

- ✔ **Last Night of Freedom:** www.lastnightoffreedom.co.uk; 0845 2602800

- ✔ **Maximise:** www.maximise.co.uk; 020 8236 0111

- ✔ **Mountain Mayhem:** www.mountainmayhem.com; 01873-860450

- ✔ **Party Bus:** www.partybus.co.uk; 0845-838-5400

- ✔ **Redseven Leisure:** www.redsevenleisure.co.uk; 0800 970 2744

- ✔ **Senor Stag:** www.senorstag.com; 01773 766052

- ✔ **The Stag Company:** www.thestagcompany.com; 01273 225 070

✔ **The Stag and Hen Company:** www.thestagandhen company.co.uk; 0844 804 5370

✔ **The Stag and Hen Experience:** www.thestagand henexperience.com; 01202 566100

✔ **Stag Party:** www.stagparty.co.uk; 01273 872230

✔ **Stagweb:** www.stagweb.co.uk; 0845-130-5225

✔ **Stag Weekends:** www.stagweekends.co.uk; 01773 766051

✔ **Superfun Stag Weekends:** www.superfunstag weekends.com

Getting Out and About

The world's your oyster. You can find activities out there for every type of stag and every type of stag do. If you don't want things to get too strenuous for your group, then what about a day of at the golf course? Or if you're after adrenalin, why not book everyone in for a parachute jump? For stag dos where all-day drinking is planned, then maybe watching rather than participating in sport is the best option. Or, organise a stag night rather than a stag day and head out clubbing.

From paintballing to parachuting

Countless companies offer stag activity days (see 'Let the pros take over' earlier in this chapter). The only problem is choosing what to do.

Keep the plan of action secret from the groom – although you may want to check with him as to what type of activity he'd like to do. Jungle training in Sierra Leone isn't everyone's cup of tea.

Bear in mind the team element of the activity. Racing cars all afternoon gets your knuckles well and truly white, but such a solo activity doesn't actually achieve what is, after all, the main purpose of the stag do: male bonding. Paintballing or a football tournament is much better for rallying everyone together.

You also have to weigh up the cost. Go-karting in Nottingham may not sound that glamorous, but this activity is a hell of a lot cheaper (and safer) than flying a MiG jet in Eastern Europe. And remember: When motorised vehicles are involved, safety is a big issue, and organisers tend to be wary about heavy drinking.

Finding out the best place near you to jump out of a plane or discovering who's got the fastest paintball guns in the West doesn't sound easy. So try the following list of contacts for a start:

- ✔ **Bungee jumping:** UK Bungee Club; www.ukbungee.co.uk; 07000 286433

- ✔ **Circus skills:** Circus Magic; http://uk.circusmagic.co.uk; 07920 400 309

- ✔ **Coasteering:** International Coasteering Association; www.coasteering.org; 0800 781 6861

- ✔ **Falconry:** Falconer's Retreat; www.falconersretreat.co.uk; 01984 634178

- ✔ **Ferrari driving:** Red Letter Days; www.redletterdays.co.uk; 0845 640 8000

- ✔ **Gliding:** British Gliding Association; www.gliding.co.uk; 0116 289 2956

- ✔ **Go-karting:** National Karting Association; www.nationalkarting.co.uk; 01206-322726

- ✔ **Hot rod driving:** Red Letter Days; www.redletterdays.co.uk; 0845 640 8000

- ✔ **Ice cricket:** Tours 4 Sport; www.icecricket.co.uk; 01869 369765

- ✔ **Kite buggying:** Extreme Academy; www.watergatebay.co.uk; 01637-860543

- ✔ **Laser gun fighting:** Laser Mission; www.laser-mission.com; 0845 373 1838

- ✔ **MiG jet flying:** Red Letter Days; www.redletterdays.co.uk; 0845 640 8000

- ✔ **Military activities:** Chillisauce; www.chillisauce.co.uk; 020 7299 1831

- ✔ **Motor sports:** Trackdays; www.trackdays.co.uk; 01376 336701

✔ **Mountain boarding:** Another World Adventure Centre; www.mountainboarding.co.uk; 01422-245196

✔ **Mountaineering:** British Mountaineering Club; www.thebmc.co.uk; 0161 445 6111;

✔ **Paintballing:** UK Paintball Sports Federation; www.ukpsf.com; 0845-130-4252

✔ **Paragliding and hang gliding:** British Hang Gliding and Paragliding Association; www.bhpa.co.uk; 0116-289-4316

✔ **Quad biking:** Quad Racing Association UK; www.qrauk.com; 07774 434468

✔ **Running with bulls in Pamplona:** PP Travel; www.pptravel.com; 020 7930 9999

✔ **Scuba diving:** British Sub-Aqua Club; www.bsac.com; 0151-350-6200

✔ **Surfing:** Surfing Great Britain; http://surfinggb.com; 07967 664643

✔ **Tank driving:** Great Experience Days; www.greatexperiencedays.co.uk; 0870-199-3355.

✔ **Wakeboarding:** Wakeboard UK; www.wakeboard.co.uk

✔ **Windsurfing:** UK Windsurfing Association; www.ukwindsurfing.com

A lot of stag activities don't mix so well with booze. Activity organisers are trained to spot or smell anyone who's had a skinful, especially if motorised vehicles are involved. Use your common sense on this one. Don't book an early morning on a racetrack if you're planning to stay up late drinking the night before.

Activity days are the perfect excuse to really have some fun at the groom's expense. Water sports require an obligatory stag dunking. Paintball always has a 'hunt the stag' option. And a military training day is just a red rag to a bull.

The groom will be expecting some form of abuse, so don't hold back. However, although nudity and handcuffs are certainly no strangers to stag dos, you don't want to stretch the groom's sense of humour too far. Avoid broken limbs and bruises. Alternatively, schedule the stag do far enough in advance of the wedding so that the groom's battered body has time to heal.

As best man, ultimately you're in charge of the groom's well-being. He may laugh as you shave off his eyebrows and chortle as you force him to undergo a tattoo. But in the cold, grey light of dawn he may not thank you for the aftermath. And once you get home, his bride-to-be will hold you personally responsible.

The Sporting Life

If the budget or the courage of the stags doesn't stretch to bungee jumping, you may want to try something a bit less nerve-straining. Team sports offer plenty of opportunities for stag bonding.

Football

Five-a-side football tournaments are held all over the United Kingdom and Europe all year round. What makes this sport so suitable for a stag do is that you can split the party into two teams and instil a bit of competition. Perhaps have the groom and bestie as skippers of the two teams. With most stag parties averaging between 10 and 15 people, this means that you've got just the right number for 2 teams of 5 plus a couple of substitutes each. And after a night of heavy drinking beforehand, you'll be very glad of those substitutes.

The following companies organise five-a-side football tournaments:

- ✔ **Goals Soccer Centres:** www.goalsfootball.co.uk

- ✔ **Sports Tours:** www.sports-tours.co.uk; 01708-336991

- ✔ **Sports Travel International:** www.stisport.com; 01279-661700

Golf

Golf may sound too pedestrian, but actually this game is the perfect stag sport. Not only can you drink all day – although do keep those hip flasks hidden until you're out of sight of the clubhouse – but you can also level the playing field by imposing handicaps. And if you split the group into teams of four, you can make things really competitive – another crucial element of any stag activity.

Here are some great ideas for variations on golf match play:

- ✔ **Best ball:** Split the group into teams of similar sizes. The winners are the team that finishes the round with the lowest score. Each team member starts off by playing his first drive. The team walks to the spot where the 'best ball' – the best of all the shots played by everyone in the whole team – lands and all play their next shot from there. They continue playing from the spot where the best ball lands each time until the first player reaches the hole. The number of shots played by this winning team member is the team's overall score.

- ✔ **Three club:** Each player chooses just three golf clubs from his bag with which to play the round. He is then forced to play with each club in strict sequence. The potential for some real course shenanigans becomes obvious as you inevitably end up putting with your driver or attempting a 100-yard drive with your sand wedge. To really spice things up, insist that everyone has the same three clubs – say a putter, a sand wedge and a driver.

- ✔ **Speed golf:** This variation is ideal for those stag parties where everyone's more interested in the 19th hole than the previous 18. Each player has just one club (say, a nine iron), and between shots he has to sprint to the ball. Points are awarded for both the time and the number of shots needed to complete each hole. When the groundsman sees 15 stags sprinting round his course, he'll be so flabbergasted that he won't even think to grumble.

For more golfing information, contact the England Golf (www.englandgolf.org; 01526-354500), Scottish Golf Union (www.scottishgolf.org; 01334-466477), Golf Union of Wales (www.golfunionwales.org; 01633-436040) or the Golfing Union of Ireland (www.gui.ie; (+353) 01-505-4000).

Golf clubs are more conservative than Margaret Thatcher. When you book your round, don't tell them that you're a stag party. The club won't even allow you to *look* at the greens, let alone play on them. Tell them that you're on a business trip instead. And behave like gentlemen . . . at least until you're all out of sight of the clubhouse.

Tenpin bowling

Opt for a bowling alley that lets you book several adjacent lanes for a whole evening. That way you can split the stag party into several teams and enjoy a bowling marathon. With tenpin bowling you don't have the problem of drinking and participating at the same time. In fact, you're normally encouraged to mix the two. Contact the British Tenpin Bowling Association for more information (www.btba.org.uk; 020-8478-1745).

On the sidelines

Spectating instead of taking part means that you don't waste valuable drinking time – and is also perfect for lazy stags. But have you ever tried to buy 15 tickets for a Premier League football match? Unless you pay through the nose for corporate hospitality, forget this idea. But worry not: Even the dullest sports events get thrilling when money's riding on the outcome. Watch croquet on the village green and the chances are you'll fall asleep before the players have negotiated the first hoop. Slap a few bets on, though, and suddenly everyone's cheering them on.

Some of the best stag dos I've been to have included a day at the races or a night at the dogs. You get the ultimate stag combo – sport, gambling, and booze. Contact the Jockey Club (www.thejockeyclub.co.uk; 020-7611-1800) or the Greyhound Board of Great Britain (www.thedogs.co.uk; 020-7421-3770) for some ideas.

Evening Entertainment

Here's where you've really got your work cut out, with so many options and so many tastes to cater for. Will the stags want to dance, gamble, admire half-naked women or just sit around and drink? You must take your lead from the groom on this. He knows the characters of his friends and can suggest how best to get them bonding and enjoying themselves.

Once you've got a plan, stick to it. And try your hardest to keep all the stags together. When you're flitting between bars and nightclubs, you can very easily lose stragglers. The more they imbibe, the more likely they are to fall by the wayside – quite literally.

Casinos: Betting you'll have a good time

Blackjack may be a bit specialist for those not used to gambling, but roulette's child's play. And what stag do is complete without a bit of risk? Although the rules governing casinos in the United Kingdom are becoming increasingly more relaxed, in most cases, you have to be a member of a casino for at least 24 hours before you're allowed to play in that casino. If you want to gain entry for the whole stag party, you're going to need to sign everyone up well in advance.

Hide the kitty before you go anywhere near a casino. After a few drinks, some bright spark always comes up with the idea of slapping the lot on black. Sod's law says that the ball lands on red.

Nightclubs: Opting for a night on the tiles

After a huge meal and inevitably too many drinks, everyone's up for shaking things around a bit. The problem is that nightclub bouncers have a natural aversion to stag parties. And who can blame them? Fifteen noisy young men are hardly likely to instil them with confidence.

You can get around this in two ways: Either call the nightclub a few days before the stag do and warn them that you'll all be turning up – on best behaviour, of course. Or, split the group into twos and threes, stagger your entry and get past Cerberus that way.

Adult clubs: Stripping down to the basics

Strip clubs aren't everyone's cup of tea. You've got to check with the groom before you make this part of the evening's action. He may be against the whole thing on principle. Or he may be worried about his bride-to-be's reaction. And yes, she's sure to find out – not everyone on the stag party can be trusted to keep shtum.

Pubs and bars: Drinking the night away

You hardly need any advice on how these work. But just one simple word of caution: If you're planning a pub crawl, make sure that you've got the mobile phone numbers of all the stags punched into your phone. That way you can reel in the inevitable stragglers.

Sorting Out the Details

Okay, so you've sat down with the groom and decided who he wants to come along and what he wants everyone to do. Now comes the tough bit: Booking everything.

If you can, try to maintain an element of surprise. As long as you're sure that the groom is happy with your destination and activities, keep the finer details secret from him. Instruct the other stags to do the same. The groom may have agreed to a weekend in Estonia, but what he doesn't know is that you're all going to be driving tanks and shooting AK47s. Little surprises like that can make his weekend all the more memorable.

Organising the finances

Get ready with the aspirin. This part is where your headache starts to kick in. Somehow, you've got to get payment from all the stag invitees so that you can book flights, hotels, activities, restaurants, bars, nightclubs. . . . And getting hefty sums of cash out of people is by no means an easy task.

To avoid upsetting any of the guests, forewarn them of every-thing they're going to have to pay for. You have already deter-mined with the groom what they can and can't afford (see 'Show me the money' earlier in this chapter), so at this stage the finances aren't up for discussion. But you can get all the stags to part with their money far more easily if you hit them with one large bill for everything rather than lots of smaller bills at separate intervals.

Email everyone in the party except the groom and explain to them exactly what they're going to have to pay for. Remember to spread out the costs of the groom between everyone else. Nowadays, the groom is not expected to pay for anything except perhaps the flight if you're travelling abroad, which is normal practice. All his other expenses should be covered by his mates.

You're expected to book everything, from the hotel and res-taurants to sporting activities and nightclubs. If you don't want to end up footing a hefty bill yourself, insist on getting payment from everyone up front. Include your bank details on the email so that they can pay the money directly into your account. You don't want to have to deal with dozens of indi-vidual cheques and wads of cash.

Paying for the flights on a foreign trip is more complicated. With budget airlines, such as easyJet, Ryanair, bmibaby and Flybe, prices vary constantly, and you're unlikely to be able to give everyone a firm quote on how much the flight is going to cost. Often, as a flight fills up, the ticket prices increase rapidly, sometimes minute by minute. To save yourself a lot of hassle, get all the stags to book their own flights. As soon as you know, tell them which flight you and the groom are on and get them to book their own seats straight away. Some quick-fingered emailing or telephoning may be necessary if you want to make sure that everyone gets on the same flight.

Here are some tips on stag trip finances:

✔ Explain in a group email exactly what everyone's paying for.

✔ Supply everyone with one total bill in advance rather than lots of smaller invoices.

> ✔ Don't forget to factor in the groom's costs.
>
> ✔ Don't book expensive services before everyone's paid.
>
> ✔ Ask everyone to book their own flights.

Don't forget to factor in how much is going to be spent on props, meals, booze, taxis and anything else that you don't normally pay for up front. Remind people to bring plenty of cash to cover these costs – see Chapter 3 for more on getting a kitty system together.

Warming up the proceedings

Now that you've got a list of all the stags' email addresses, send regular updates. You find that as the stag do approaches, everyone indulges in a bit of email banter – and what a good way to break the ice and put the wind up the groom!

In the days just before the stag party, you want to keep everyone in close communication so that proceedings get off to a good start. Send reminders about where you're meeting and what essentials people need to bring. For a weekend in Prague, you may need walking boots, clothes for running around the woods and getting 'shot' and smart gear for the nightclub. However much you prime all the guests though, you can guarantee that someone is going to turn up unprepared.

Get the mobile phone numbers of everyone involved and plug them into your own phone. You need these to rally the troops on the day that you all meet up.

Clothing the stag

Dressing up the groom so that he looks like a prize idiot is considered standard behaviour on the stag night. Before you all meet up for the start of the stag party, pay a quick visit to a charity shop. Most high streets in Britain have at least one, so you should be spoilt for choice. Here, you're guaranteed to discover a glut of tasteless out-of-date clothing. Ideally, you want the groom dressed in drag: Old tights and a 1980s floral dress goes down a treat. If you can find high heels in his size, all the better.

Some stags try to wriggle out of wearing a stupid outfit. On no account should you let this happen. He's got no choice. He's expected to stand out as an object of derision, and it's the job of the other stags to enforce this. (Chapter 3 has more ideas for setting up the groom.)

Let's be civil

With more and more same-sex UK couples getting hitched, there's a chance you may be best man for a gay couple. Civil partnerships and same-sex marriages haven't been around for long in this country, so gay stag parties don't have the same centuries-old traditions as straight ones. In fact, many gay couples don't bother with a stag party at all, choosing instead to do all the partying at the post-nuptial reception. Those who do opt for a stag party tend to make it a joint one, with all their mutual friends (male or female) invited along. The basic elements are the same: Celebrate the end of both men's bachelorhoods with lots of booze and revelry. The only major difference is that the bumps on the strippers will be in different places.

Chapter 3

The Stag Party

*A*rranging a stag do used to be so simple. You'd just book the restaurant and work out a good route for a pub crawl – easier than the proverbial gathering in a brewery. But for the modern stag party, all has changed. Most grooms expect something a lot more adventurous, a lot more exciting and perhaps even a lot more foreign.

This expectation doesn't make your job as best man any easier. Fifteen rowdy stags on the high street of a provincial town are just about manageable. Throw in air travel, suspicious hotel managers and an alien language, and suddenly you've got a lot more on your hands than you bargained for.

A bit of military planning is in order. The best man has to be highly organised so that the rest of the stags can enjoy themselves without thinking. So work out a plan and do your utmost to stick to it.

Warming Up the Stags

An air of expectation builds up before the stag party officially starts. In most cases, the majority of stags already know one another. Those stags who don't – usually the group has a couple of old or distant friends – can glean vital information from all the banter in the weeks running up to the party. (Refer to Chapter 2 for more on pre-party communication.) But you still want to get things off to a good start – not so much a case of breaking the ice as warming things up a bit.

Where is the group going to meet? Pubs are the obvious starting points. Get everyone to agree to arrive on time at the first watering hole. You need to choose a convenient one. If you're all going to be travelling together across country from the same city to the stag destination, then pick a bar that everyone can find easily. Or, if you've got room in the budget, why not book a limousine to transport you all? Yes, sounds cheesy, but this idea can result in a lot less hassle and sometimes works out cheaper than long-distance train fares for all of you. Limos come with fridges, tinted windows and a bit of rock-star attitude. And the forced proximity has you all bonding in no time.

Pubs near or in railway stations tend to be about as much fun as the station toilets. If you're simply meeting up, this kind of public house shouldn't pose a problem. But if you plan to spend any time there, then you may want to opt for a nicer drinking hole a short walk away.

But what about foreign stag trips? Airports aren't the world's most delightful meeting points, especially on busy Friday evenings. Concourse bars can be grim, so for a bit of style, why not book everyone into the business or first-class lounge? Even though you're no doubt all flying cattle class, this doesn't exclude you from a bit of pampering. These lounges are always well stocked with refreshments – just what the expectant stags need.

If you book everyone into a posh airport lounge, don't make the fact that you're on a stag trip obvious, as the staff are highly likely to refuse you entry. And go easy on the drinking – even if the booze is free. With all the security measures in place at airports, airlines won't hesitate to keep drunkards off the plane – especially, if you have 15 rowdy male drunkards.

No Sleep 'Til . . .

Whether the stag do is one evening or a whole weekend, the party's all about momentum. You're the best man, and you need to keep the bash going. Printing an itinerary is a great idea so that all the stags know what's happening and when. Keep them as busy as you can. On a weekend do, no one, least of all you, wants to get up early. But organise full afternoon activities on both days if you can.

The evening's activities are even more important than those in the afternoon, so give extra thought to what you're going to be doing. If you don't stick to your original course of action (drinks, dinner, more drinks, nightclub, taxi home – or whatever), some of the more strong-headed stags may suggest alternative plans, which is a really bad idea: Deviation causes arguments and may split up the group. Stick to your agenda and make the evening bash work.

Getting 'em in

One area that can really test your diplomatic skills is buying drinks. With a group of 10 or 15 stags, you're going to have drinkers of different speeds and different tastes. If you're not careful, problems can arise, especially if a lot of the stags don't know each other well.

You may find that getting everyone to chip in for every round is impractical – nay, impossible – so you can avoid arguments by implementing a *kitty system*. At the start of the evening ask everyone for enough money for, say, ten drinks (the groom, of course, gets free drinks all night). Put all the money into one wallet and keep it safe in your pocket. This wallet becomes the official kitty and covers all drinks bought throughout the evening. If things really get going, you may need to top up the cash later.

At the start of the night, try to gauge how much cash you're going to need for everyone's drinks. And remember, people aren't necessarily going to complain about the amount of money that they have to stump up – but they can if you ask them too often. Believe me, you'll be far more popular if you ask for a one-off contribution of £50 each rather than three smaller contributions at different stages during the evening.

Remember to include costs of drinks in your initial requests for money (check out Chapter 2 for more on this). But, no matter how well you judge what's going to be spent on booze, averaging the cost out between stags is never necessarily going to be fair. I'm afraid this is just part and parcel of a good stag night. Although the lads from the groom's rugby club won't think twice about downing five pints in an hour, Tiny Tim from accounts may take all evening to nurse a small white wine spritzer. Financially, slow drinkers are always going to get a raw deal.

Everyone drinks at a different speed, which means that, even with a kitty system, the slower drinkers inevitably feel that they haven't had their money's worth by the end of the night. You can get around this by having two kitties – one for the hard-core drinkers and one for the lightweights.

Carrying on after hours

What often happens is that a hard-core contingent, including the groom and the best man, stays up until the wee hours. Those who need their beauty sleep or who want to throw in the towel can do so when the kitty runs out – with no shame attached. The iron-livered stags, meanwhile, can start a new kitty and see the party through until dawn. This second kitty is the one that inevitably ends up paying for luxuries like brandy and cigars.

Setting Him Up

No stag night is complete without some practical jokes at the groom's expense. You don't want to take things too far (a plaster cast and an arm in a sling don't look good at the altar), but at the same time, you don't want to let the groom get off too lightly. He will, after all, be expecting a bit of gentle humiliation. Here are a few ideas:

  ✔ **Ridiculous clothing:** High-street charity shops offer a wonderful selection of nasty floral dresses and old tights. (Refer to Chapter 2 for more on sourcing sartorial masterpieces.)

✔ **Rude props:** Joke shops stock no end of amusing inflatable items. Yes, they're immature, but they're also exceedingly funny in the right situations.

✔ **Stripograms:** Pretend policewomen, titillating traffic wardens and any number of other variations can be fun for the whole party.

✔ **Public humiliation:** Handcuffing the groom and leaving him to stew for a while is always popular. But let him keep his underpants on so that he doesn't get arrested for indecent exposure. The aforementioned police officer will gladly help.

Don't take the practical jokes too far. The purpose of any punishment you inflict on the groom is to make everyone laugh, not cry – including the groom. So avoid jokes that end up leaving long-term evidence or that the bride can find out about. Handcuffing the groom half-naked to a lamppost may only injure his pride. But bruises, broken limbs and shaved eyebrows could still be in evidence when he takes his wedding vows.

Getting the Stag Home

In the latter stages of the stag do, your role starts to shift from being a travel guide to being a babysitter. A night of revelry can take its toll on the poor groom, and you must be there to pick up the pieces.

On many stag parties, the groom finds himself under huge peer pressure to consume tanker-loads of alcohol. He may have trouble simply remembering his name, let alone how he's going to get home at the end of the bash. As best man, you're there to metaphorically hold his hand. You must remain clear-headed enough to moderate the groom's intake and get him home and tucked up in bed safely.

No one's expecting you to stay sober during the stag party – what a preposterous suggestion. As maître d', you're expected to get the party going. But best not to get blind drunk. You're in charge of the proceedings and ensuring that nothing goes wrong is your responsibility – very hard to do if you've passed out, lost the kitty and woken up in jail.

A lot of stag parties take place in the groom's home town. If the groom lives with his bride-to-be, this can be a recipe for disaster. At the end of the night, with a bellyful of booze inside him, he may feel a little amorous and try to get home to his loved one – which is a very bad idea, so don't let him near her. If she sees or smells him after a night on the tiles with all the other stags, she may just go off the whole idea of marrying him. Don't even let him call her. The future bride and groom must never spend the night of the stag do together. If absolutely necessary, send her a reassuring text message at the end of the night.

Dealing with Emergencies

In certain cities in the United Kingdom (Blackpool, Brighton, Nottingham, Newquay) and abroad (Prague, Barcelona, Tallinn, Vilnius), stag parties are so common that they've become part of the furniture. This fact doesn't mean that you're allowed to get away with breaking the law. Although the local police officers may simply wag a few fingers when the party gets a bit out of control, their job is to keep the peace. Push them too far, and you may all spend a night in the cells – not much fun if the groom's wearing comedy breasts and a tight floral print dress. As best man, your job is to keep everyone out of trouble.

Here are some tips on how to avoid, or extricate yourselves from, nightmare stag-party scenarios:

- **Your name's not on the list:** Bouncers at bars and nightclubs are under strict instructions not to allow big groups of drunken men into their establishments. You need to call up the manager the week before to clear the way or approach the club in small groups. You can all join up again when you're inside.

- **Air rage:** If the stag weekend involves air travel, be sure to keep everyone sober before lift-off. Security staff don't look kindly on rowdy passengers and are likely to bump you off the flight if you smell like a distillery. Most cheap flights are now unticketed, so arrive at the departure gates early if you want to sit together.

✔ **Diner's card:** Have you ever been in a restaurant enjoying a quiet meal with your partner when a 15-strong stag party troops in and occupies the adjacent table? This scenario can be funny for the first few minutes, but when the food fights start, the tempers of the other diners may start to fray a little. When checking out restaurants, ask whether they have private dining rooms. Behind closed doors, the stag party can forget about table manners and civilised society.

✔ **No groom at the inn:** You don't want the groom passing out before the party's over. And what use is a stag celebration that he barely remembers? Some of the other stags may see this as an opportunity to really stitch up the poor bloke by pouring drinks down his neck. You're there to make sure that they don't go too far. One way to do this is to instigate the 'He drinks only what you drink' rule.' You insist that whatever the others buy for the groom, they must also consume themselves. This rule cuts down on the number of lethal cocktails he has to swallow.

✔ **Home, James:** Sadly, every stag evening comes to the point when you really have to get the groom to bed – for his own good, if nothing else. Arm yourself with the numbers of several local cab firms before the evening starts so that when the time comes, you can make the ending quick and painless.

✔ **A cache of cash:** The kitty is sure to run out quicker than you think. And on a weekend night in the centre of a large town, so are the cashpoint machines. Always keep a couple of large notes stashed on your person for emergencies.

Putting the Party on Record

Many of the group are going to have very tender heads indeed after the stag do. The groom, especially, will need a few days to recover. He may also need to work his way gently back into his fiancée's good books. But don't lose the momentum you all created during the stag do. You still have a few post-stag duties to fulfil.

Taking photographic evidence

After a suitable rest period, contact all the stags and ask them to send you copies of the best photos from the party. Keep all the pictures together. If they're suitable for general viewing, you may want to put them in a stag-party photo album and present them to the groom on his wedding day. Do him and his new wife a favour, though, and leave out the smutty pics.

Take care, though: Cameras can be a liability on a stag do. In the wrong hands, they create all sorts of troublesome evidence that may come back later to haunt the groom.

Don't ban cameras altogether, as the stag do is bound to have some superb photographic opportunities. However, what you can do is ask the other stags not to take cameras out with them during the evening's entertainment.

Getting the stag online

Setting up a website dedicated to the stag do is a great idea. If computers aren't your strong point, try to persuade one of the more tech-savvy stags to set up a website displaying the funnier episodes of the bash. Use a password to prevent the bride from seeing what she shouldn't.

Try all the obvious social media websites, such as Facebook, YouTube, Myspace, Bebo and the like. But if you want to keep things simple, why not just upload all the (decent) stag party photos or onto a photo-sharing or video-sharing website?

The following photo-sharing websites offer a free or very cheap service. Add a few funny captions, and you've made a great memento for everyone involved:

- ✔ www.flickr.com
- ✔ http://imageshack.us
- ✔ http://memeo.com
- ✔ http://beta.photobucket.com

✔ http://pinterest.com

✔ http://picasa.google.com

✔ www.photobox.co.uk

Video-sharing websites:

✔ http://YouTube.com

✔ http://Blip.tv

✔ http://Vimeo.com

✔ www.viddler.com

✔ www.dailymotion.com

Part II
Wedding Preparations and the Big Day

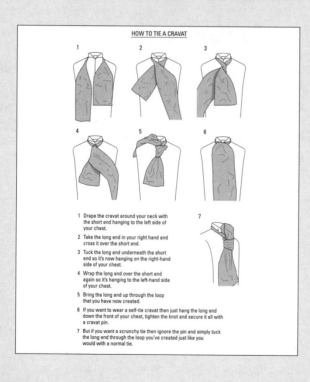

HOW TO TIE A CRAVAT

1   2   3

4   5   6

1 Drape the cravat around your neck with the short end hanging to the left side of your chest.

2 Take the long end in your right hand and cross it over the short end.

3 Tuck the long end underneath the short end so it's now hanging on the right-hand side of your chest.

4 Wrap the long end over the short end again so it's hanging to the left-hand side of your chest.

5 Bring the long end up through the loop that you have now created.

6 If you want to wear a self-tie cravat then just hang the long end down the front of your chest, tighten the knot and secure it all with a cravat pin.

7 But if you want a scrunchy tie then ignore the pin and simply tuck the long end through the loop you've created just like you would with a normal tie.

7

In this part . . .

- ✓ Map out all the details for the big day so that you can play your part in the wedding preparations.

- ✓ Know how to handle the ceremony by being prepared for every detail, such as keeping the ring safe, seating people and signing the all-important official paperwork.

- ✓ Find out how to get all the guests to the reception, meet and greet and coordinate pictures.

Chapter 4

The Build-Up to the Big Day

*A*s the big day gets closer and closer, your duties mount up rapidly. You may have spent the past few months focusing on the stag party (check out Chapters 2 and 3) and material for your speech (I wax lyrical about this in Chapters 8 and 9). But now the time has come to get your head around the intricacies of the wedding ceremony and the reception.

As the bride and groom start bombarding you with questions about buttonholes, receiving lines and signing the register, you may suddenly be struck by the full gravity of the situation: One of your best friends is getting married, and he and his bride – or their families – are shelling out thousands of pounds to make the day one that no one forgets.

Be sure that you fulfil your side of the bargain: Stay calm, be organised and keep lists, and the day is going to go swimmingly.

Getting Him to the Church on Time

Getting the groom to the venue before the ceremony is down to you. For most weddings, this means one of two things:

✔ The groom chooses to hire a special car for the whole day, in which case he may ask you to drive him to the ceremony and be ready to help out with any mechanical problems should they arise (the mainstay of many a sitcom wedding).

✔ Except in very unusual circumstances, you drive the groom to the ceremony in your own vehicle. Nerves may prevent him from holding a steering wheel, let alone actually controlling a vehicle, so whatever you do don't let the groom drive himself.

Keep a list of local taxi firms handy in case disaster strikes, and the car breaks down.

✔ If the groom doesn't want to hire a special car and your own vehicle isn't reliable, then book a taxi in advance to take you both to the wedding venue.

(Cruise over to Chapter 5 for more on getting to the wedding venue, hassle free.).

You need to arrive at the wedding venue at least an hour and a half before the other guests to check that everything's in order and have time to share a premarital drink with the groom and ushers.

After the happy couple is hitched, the groom becomes in charge of the car that whisks them away to the reception. This one probably won't be the same car that you both arrived in earlier – more likely to be the vehicle in which the bride and her father arrived at the venue – so you may be required to drive it yourself to the reception.

Preparing Your Wedding Wardrobe

Although a bit of sartorial advice won't be wasted on your groom, really you have to take your lead from the wedding couple. They may simply tell you what you're going to wear. If they give you a choice, you quite literally follow suit. Groom, bestie and ushers all kitted out in matching suits certainly turns heads.

If the bride and groom are leaving you to your own devices, don't panic. This section gives you a quick overview of the most popular bestie wedding outfits, and then I offer a few dressing suggestions for sartorial splendour. Just remember not to show up the bride.

As best man, you're the third most admired member of the wedding party. So make an effort!

Choosing your garb

The bride and groom may have decided on a very formal wedding with morning suits, waistcoats and cravats. Or perhaps the groom wants you and all his ushers in white – in which case, don't spill the red wine. If you're Scottish and normally wear a kilt to weddings, you're unwise to assume that a sporran and no underpants fit in with the groom's plans. (See the sidebar 'Suits you, Sir!' for a list of the best wedding suit suppliers.)

Take time out to discuss all the options with the bride and groom. Don't go independent and just turn up on the big day with a little surprise. You don't want to look ridiculous or scruffy. Nor do you want to upstage the groom with a bespoke Savile Row outfit.

Morning suits

This classic British ensemble has made something of a comeback in recent years. Morning suits may be considered old-fashioned by some, but in reality they're timeless and work in most occasions, whether you're tying the knot at Westminster Abbey, West Ham registry office or a village church in the West Highlands.

Ever since Hugh Grant showcased the traditional English wedding in *Four Weddings and a Funeral,* waistcoats have become fashionable again. Waistcoats are supposed to be a bit of fun and add a dash of colour to the dark grey of the suit, but my advice is to play safe and opt for sober colours, such as buff, gold, or grey. Mickey Mouse or Homer Simpson prints are not a good idea. And always opt for linen or cotton: On a summer's day, you're going to be quite warm enough in your suit.

Keep the shirt simple – stick to plain white – and go for a solid collar that won't wilt as the day progresses.

This is repeated in appendix – delete from appendix

Suits you, Sir!

Don't take any chances when hiring your wedding suit. Here are some of the best outlets:

✔ **Anthony Formalwear:** Very modern and even a bit over the top, if that's what you're after (www. anthonyformalwear. co.uk; 01277-651140).

✔ **Hugh Harris:** Based in Woking, Surrey, this company is small but very experienced. They stock some designer names, too (www.hughharris.co.uk; 01483 756267).

✔ **Moss Bros Hire:** The biggest company in the game, with over 130 stores nationwide. The prices are great value, too (www.moss.co.uk).

✔ **Neal & Palmer:** From Nehru jackets to frockcoats and morning suits, this Jermyn Street shop stocks 'em all (www.nealand palmer.com; 020-7495-4094).

✔ **21st Century Kilts:** The Scots among you can try this Edinburgh-based hire shop (www.21stcenturykilts. com).

✔ **Young's Hire:** Dozens of concessions across the UK and Ireland (www.youngs-hire. co.uk).

✔ **Swarbrick's Formal Hire:** This Manchester-based outlet has a huge showroom and every type of wedding suit on offer (www. swarbricks.co.uk; 0161 643 4040).

Other suits

If the wedding is not strictly formal, you have more scope when choosing your outfit. Saying that, you can't just rock up in the suit you were wearing to work the day before.

If he can afford to, the groom may hire matching suits for the best man and ushers. At the very least, he probably wants his best man dolled up similarly to him. Considering all the other expenses he's crying over, you may want to help him out by paying for the hire of your own suit. Raise the matter delicately and early on in the planning process. Refer to Chapter 1 for a detailed best man's timetable.

Black tie is another option. Traditionally, a wedding requires morning rather than evening dress. Certainly, tuxedoes and bow ties can look a bit strange in an English country church-yard. But if the ceremony is late afternoon and the reception doesn't start until sundown, why not?

Weighed down by all the pressure of the wedding preparations, some grooms tend to lose all fashion sense. Suddenly, the groom has ideas about getting married all in pink and expects the best man to follow suit. Think of the wedding photos: You've got to put your foot down and give him a dose of the fashion police. And if he won't listen to you, get his bride involved.

Neckties

Whatever kind of suit you choose, keep the tie simple and traditional. Dark and plain or with a very discreet pattern is best. Try to match with the colour in your waistcoat and cufflinks if you're wearing them. If you want to wear a cravat, you have to wear one with a morning suit (see the section 'Cool cat in a cravat' later on). With evening dress, have a bit of class and get a real rather than a clip-on bowtie.

Buttonholes

Buttonholes aren't actually the holes you secure your suit buttons through: They're a piece of floral finery designed for wearing on your lapel (in the buttonhole – clever, eh?). The flower of choice is usually a carnation or rose and in most cases is supplied to groom, bestie and all the ushers by the wedding florist. The flowers are delivered to the bride's mother on the morning of the wedding, and so you need to instruct one of the ushers to collect the ones allocated to your group. You then distribute them when you and the groom meet up with the ushers (head to Chapter 5 for more on preparing the ushers on the big day). If a buttonhole hasn't already been arranged for you then make a quick call to a local florist. But make sure that the bride approves your choice. Buttonholes both look smart and also signal to confused guests that you're a person they can direct questions at. Whether you can answer them or not. . . . Well, that's why you're reading this book.

Top hats and trimmings

Overzealous salespeople may try to bamboozle you into hiring all the optional extras with your morning suit. Beware!

Morning dress should look classy, not daft. If you have any choice in what you're wearing, keep the outfit simple.

Top hats, gloves, canes, spats and – dare I say – monocles make you look more like a clown than a best man. You're bound to break them or lose them, along with a hefty deposit. A top hat may be particularly tempting, but believe me: You're only going to wear it only for the photos. The rest of the day you end up carrying that hat around. Or big Auntie Ethel sits on it.

Wearing your kit correctly

Getting the correct clothing together is one thing. Wearing the outfit correctly is another, particularly when formal dress is the order of the day.

Morning suits

Morning dress takes a lot of nous to get right. Even the toffs mess things up occasionally. Prince William often used to turn up to weddings smothered in a morning coat way too big for him. Presumably his father paid so much for the jacket that he thought he'd let the lad grow into it.

The suit jacket should fit snugly around the chest and shoulders, which should be reinforced with some minimal padding. Even off-the-peg jackets are tailored ever so slightly differently from one another, so don't be afraid to try on dozens before you choose the right one. The jacket should meet across your abdomen without straining or overlapping too much. Just remember the effects of canapés, dinner and wedding cake. Etiquette states that the button remains undone. The tails should hang in length nearly to the back of your knees.

Cool cat in a cravat

Cravats are worn only with morning suits. Tying one is a lot trickier than you think. Figure 4-1 shows you how to tie a cravat properly.

HOW TO TIE A CRAVAT

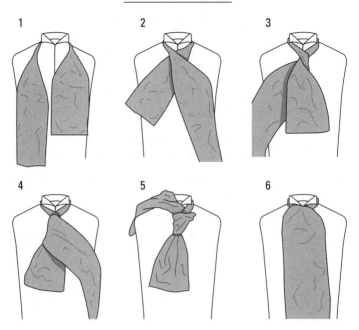

1 Drape the cravat around your neck with the short end hanging to the left side of your chest.

2 Take the long end in your right hand and cross it over the short end.

3 Tuck the long end underneath the short end so it's now hanging on the right-hand side of your chest.

4 Wrap the long end over the short end again so it's hanging to the left-hand side of your chest.

5 Bring the long end up through the loop that you have now created.

6 If you want to wear a self-tie cravat then just hang the long end down the front of your chest, tighten the knot and secure it all with a cravat pin.

7 But if you want a scrunchy tie then ignore the pin and simply tuck the long end through the loop you've created just like you would with a normal tie.

Figure 4-1: Tying a cravat.

1. **Wrap the cravat around your neck.**

   The short end should hang down the left side of your chest.

2. **With your right hand, grab the long end and cross it over the short end.**

3. **Tuck the long end beneath the short end so that the long end is now hanging down the right side of your chest.**

4. **Wrap the long end over the short end again so that the long end now hangs on the left side of your chest.**

5. **Stuff the long end up through the loop that you've made.**

6. **Finish up neatly.**

   For a self-tie cravat, simply hang the long end down your chest, tighten the knot and secure it with a cravat pin.

   If you want a scrunchy cravat, then knot the long end through the loop you've made, just as you would with a normal tie.

Practise tying your cravat before the big day. And make sure that the groom knows what he's doing with his.

Bow constrictor

Nothing looks smarter than a well-tied bow tie. A bow tie is essential if the bride and groom have opted for evening wear. The step-by-step guide in Figure 4-2 shows you how to tie the bow correctly.

1. **Loop the tie round your neck, with one end a little longer than the other.**

2. **Tuck the long end up through the loop to make a tie.**

3. **Double the short end over itself to make the front loop of the tie.**

   Let the long end drop down over this loop.

4. **Now double the long end over itself to make the second loop of the tie; push this second loop through the first.**

5. **Tighten the knot by adjusting the ends of both loops.**

HOW TO TIE A BOW TIE

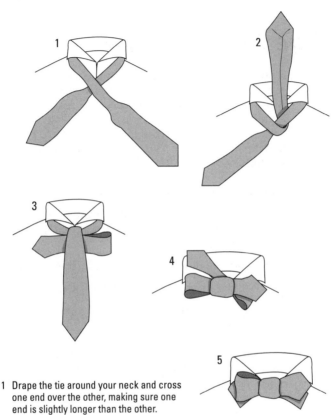

1 Drape the tie around your neck and cross one end over the other, making sure one end is slightly longer than the other.

2 Bring the long end up through the loop you've created.

3 Double the short end over itself to create the front base loop of the bow tie. Drop the long end down over this base loop.

4 While holding everything in place, double the long end back on itself to create the second loop of the bow tie. Then poke it through the loop behind the bow tie.

5 Adjust the bow tie by tugging at the ends and straightening the central knot. Don't worry if it's not perfectly symmetrical. All the best bow ties are ever so slightly askew. It proves that they're not clip-ons.

Figure 4-2: Tying a bow-tie.

Don't worry if it's not perfectly symmetrical.

As with all of your wedding clothing, make sure that you've had a practice run before the morning of the ceremony.

Ushering the Ushers

As best man, you're in charge of the ushers. Normally, ushers are close friends of the groom and perhaps one of the bride's brothers. Without them, the wedding seating would almost certainly turn into something of a bun fight, and the guests' cars would end up parked all over the shop. The ushers' most important duties (and you can read about these in more detail in Chapter 5) are

- Seating everyone at the wedding venue.
- Ensuring that the guests' cars are parked with some semblance of order, at both the wedding venue and the reception.
- Handing out orders of service to the guests.
- Helping to organise people for the wedding photographs.
- Directing all the guests from the wedding venue to the reception.

These duties may sound fairly simple, but you have to keep tabs on things and work out with the bride and groom a *wedding schedule* (head to Chapter 5 for more on this item) giving details of who does what and when. Then, your job is to pass on this information to the ushers. You can send an email or telephone the ushers several days in advance to brief them of their duties, which slightly takes the pressure off you rather than waiting until the morning of the wedding.

Most grooms appoint a *chief usher*. If your groom hasn't done this, encourage him to do so since the chief usher removes a lot of weight off your already sagging shoulders. His role is simply to oversee the duties of all the other ushers. A successful wedding day inevitably requires some sensible delegation.

Check that all the ushers know who sits where during the ceremony. As a general rule, heading toward the registrar, the bride's family and guests are on the left and the groom's party are on the right. The more important the guests, the nearer the front they should sit. (Chapter 6 has the details on a traditional seating plan.)

After the ceremony, the ushers direct all the guests to the reception and show them where to park. Always leave one usher behind to pick up the stragglers.

Rehearsing the Wedding Ceremony

Normally held a few days before the wedding, the dress rehearsal is everyone's chance to iron out any last-minute problems and confirm exactly what they're expected to do. The rehearsal is a valuable opportunity for you to have a clear idea in your mind of what your duties at the ceremony are. The bride and groom create a wedding schedule and if they haven't already done so they should now pass you a copy of this timetable. (Head to Chapter 5 for an idea of what a wedding schedule looks like.)

Understanding the ceremony

Normally, the bride, her father, the groom and his best man – you, remember! – take a walk through the ceremony with the minister or registrar. You discover

- ✔ Where and when to stand and sit
- ✔ The running order of the ceremony
- ✔ The vows that the couple are going to take

Wear ordinary clothes to the rehearsal. The wedding party, especially the bride, won't want anyone to see their outfits before the real ceremony.

Make the most of the rehearsal. This occasion may be the first time that you've ever seen the venue, so familiarise yourself with

- ✔ Where the toilets and exits are, so you know where to send guests if they need to know
- ✔ The layout of the car park
- ✔ Where the ushers should stand as the guests file in
- ✔ Where you and the groom stand
- ✔ Lines of sight for the photographer if there are to be photographs at the venue
- ✔ Any possible obstructions to the bride's entrance or exit

Now that you've got an idea of the size and shape of the venue, revisit the wedding schedule. Does the timing of the agenda seem realistic?

Playing the part

In a way, you're on ceremony of sorts during the rehearsal. Although they might not let on, the bride and her family are going to be monitoring you to check that you're not going to make a mess of things on the big day itself. Reassure them by taking the rehearsal seriously. Prove to them again that you are indeed the right man for the job. At this late stage, they can't do much if you're not – but reassure them anyway.

By all means, make constructive suggestions regarding the duties of you and the ushers. But don't try to modify any other part of the ceremony. You may think the music that the bride and groom have chosen is utterly naff. You may wonder how on earth the bride's mother is going to squeeze through the doors of the venue. But your place is not to change key aspects of the wedding. Just pay attention and do what you're told.

At this stage, the groom won't have much say in the mechanics of the actual ceremony. Nor will the father of the bride – even if he's paying for the whole thing. By this point, the only people who call the shots are the bride and her mother. Sorry, but that's just the way of things.

Yes, minister

Whoever the couple have chosen to marry them – vicar, priest, rabbi, mullah, registrar, druid – he wants the ceremony to run smoothly and correctly. The last thing he needs is for the service to feature on *You've Been Framed!* For this reason, he looks for reassurance during the wedding rehearsal that all the key players know exactly what their roles are.

The rehearsal may be your first chance to meet the minister or registrar. Go that bit extra to connect with him, and let him know that you've got things under control. Get him on your side by acting responsibly and with suitable reverence. Then, when the big day comes around, everything is easier for all of you.

May all your problems be little ones

Some weddings feature pageboys or very young bridesmaids. They may be at the rehearsal, perhaps with their parents. Little kids add charm and a certain unpredictability to the ceremony – and can even shed a few tears. Fortunately, the parents are there to deal with the worst problems. However, as best man, you certainly have some responsibility to check that the pageboys behave themselves.

 Learn the names of the little ones and remember who their parents are. If a tantrum occurs on the wedding day, you need all your powers of diplomacy to keep things cool. A few bribing sweets wouldn't go amiss either.

 In all the pre-nuptial fracas you may well forget to buy a wedding present for the bride and groom. (In fact, given the contribution you are making to their big day by being best man, they would both probably forgive the oversight.) Try to buy them something original, even if you end up purchasing from the official wedding list. Or perhaps you might go off-piste and buy them a more personal gift.

Organising the Groom's Last Night

Just possibly – nay, highly probably – the groom is going to get very nervous the night before his wedding. As the groom is now well past the point of no return, your job as best man is to bolster his spirits and keep him relaxed. Make sure that the groom knows that you're taking good care of everything.

The last supper

A long-established tradition in the United States, this idea is now becoming more commonplace this side of the Atlantic. The final dinner takes place the evening before the wedding. You can arrange the meal in two ways:

- All the main players in the wedding party (bride, groom, both sets of parents, bridesmaids, best man, ushers, close family) get together for a big dinner – a last chance to bond before the big day. This event may take place at the bride's family home or a nearby restaurant.

- The groom, his best man and all the ushers meet up to celebrate, in a fairly restrained way, the groom's last meal as a free man. In a way, this get together is a mini stag party – but without all the booze and raucous behaviour. This meeting is a good chance for the groom to do his final bonding with his closest friends. He can also take this opportunity to discuss, on a fairly serious level, his imminent departure from bachelorhood. Let's face facts: There probably wasn't much serious discussion on the stag do.

I favour the second option. The wedding couple can meet up with both sets of parents plenty of times once they're married, but when will the groom ever get the chance again to dine as a single man with all his best friends? Let the groom decide.

You're the one making the big speech the following day, so no one expects you to orate during the last supper. But if all the boys together, you may as well have a few words ready. Just some best wishes and a toast will suffice. Save your best wit and rhetoric for the reception.

Don't let the groom imbibe too much the night before the wedding. You don't want him staggering bleary-eyed up the aisle, stinking of a brewery. And lay off the sauce yourself. You both should have done all your drinking at the stag party.

The last-minute details

If you're both staying at the groom's place the night before the wedding, then that keeps accommodation arrangements simple. But weddings are quite often held in the bride's home town, in which case you and the groom may need to book a hotel. Arranging this part is normally the groom's responsibility. However, his nerves can be so delicate that you ought to check that you've both got a place to stay.

Don't book in to separate hotels. You're the one who has to get the groom up bright and early for his big day. This is going to be very tricky if you're halfway across town on a busy Saturday morning.

The final checklist

The day before the wedding is your last chance to get everything you need. You're going to be far too busy to nip down the shops before the ceremony.

- ✔ **Alarm clocks:** No lie-ins on the big day.
- ✔ **Mobile phone:** Make sure that you charge it to the max.
- ✔ **Wallet:** Have you got loads of cash?
- ✔ **Clothing:** Have you and the groom ironed your shirts and hung up your clothing? Don't forget ties and waistcoats.
- ✔ **Transport:** All set for tomorrow morning?
- ✔ **The ring:** Make the groom show you where he's keeping it safe.

Chapter 5

The Morning of the Wedding

The day of reckoning is here. You feel as if only yesterday the groom first asked you to be best man, and yet here you are, standing beside one of your best friends, guiding him into married life.

Weddings inevitably feature the unexpected, which is what makes them so unforgettable. Be ready to think on your feet – not everything's going to go to plan. If you remember this, you can be ready for anything.

Rise and Shine

A single alarm clock is not sufficient. Today is not a day for lie-ins. You need an alarm for each ear – and then one for luck.

The best man may well stay with the groom the night before the wedding, and I highly recommend this. (Check out Chapter 4 for more on arranging the groom's last night before the wedding.) Not only can you allay any last-minute nerves, but you can also make sure that on the biggest day of his life, the groom's up in time, bright-eyed and bushy-tailed.

If, for some reason, you're staying elsewhere from the groom (very inadvisable), then call him several times throughout the morning to check on his progress. Any oversleeping is your fault.

Cool as a Cucumber

The morning of the wedding is a time for coolness and calm. Don't let the nerves battle their way in. Not only must you keep your own mental state under control, but you must also ensure that the groom is a model of composure. The groom is about to embark on the biggest day of his life – and your job is to make sure that all goes smoothly (see Figure 5-1).

The groom's bound to be nervous. His mind is all over the shop, and his legs may be quaking like Elvis Presley's. You may even have to help him get dressed. You're the one who is going to drive him to the wedding (cross over to 'Crosstown Traffic' later in his chapter). Don't forget that in all things today, from the car to the ceremony, you – yes, that's *you*! – are the groom's right-hand man.

Talk to the groom throughout the morning in calm, reassuring terms. Try to act as if everything's normal. Get him to focus on the enjoyable aspects of his wedding day:

- ✔ He's joining forces with the love of his life, and this beautiful, kind, intelligent (embellish somewhat as necessary) woman is going to make him happy forever.

- ✔ He looks a million dollars in his stunning wedding suit. Everyone at the do's going to admire him as he strides up the aisle. Tell him that all the female guests will fancy him, and all the male guests will be jealous of how cool he looks.

- ✔ He's going to make a witty, confident speech that is going to get his new wife all mushy. Remind him how lucky he is that his speech needs to be only a few minutes long, while yours is the main performance.

- ✔ Remind him what a stupendous party you're all going to have at the reception.

This schedule assumes that the wedding is taking place around 3pm. Use it as a guide, and use your common sense.

8AM
Wake up and turn off your alarm clock. And the other one. And then *stay* awake.

8.05AM
Wake the groom. If you're staying in separate places, phone him. Make sure he's up and moving.

8.30AM
Carry out a last-minute check of the travel arrangements. If you're driving, make sure the car starts. If you're going by cab, make sure they haven't lost the booking.

9AM
Make sure you have the clothing (all of it), money, and paperwork. And above all, the ring (or rings)...

Morning
Collect the buttonholes and Orders of Service from the bride's house.

3 Hours Before the Wedding
Meet up at the wedding venue with the groom and the ushers. Have a final run-through which usher is responsible for what. Check again that you have the ring.

2 Hours Before
If you're having a last drink, pop to the local for it now. And just the one.

1 Hour Before
Get to the church or registry office and prepare to meet the guests as they arrive

10 Minutes Before
Check the ring again. Check the emergency spare.

5 Minutes Before
Take your place on the groom's right at the front of the venue.

Figure 5-1: The prelude to the wedding

If you can get the groom to the ceremony with as little stress as possible, he's going to be more confident about tying the knot. Shield him from the tension and worry of the wedding day and let him focus on his most important task: marrying his bride.

Cross-Town Traffic

Weddings held in small villages tend to be logistically very simple. No traffic, no parking restrictions – just turn up and waltz on in. But city weddings can be a transport nightmare – think tailbacks, traffic wardens, one-way systems and gawping tourists, to name but a few problems.

Whatever you do, don't leave yourselves a long journey on the morning of the wedding day. Ideally, you're accompanying the groom to the venue anyway (see 'Rise and Shine', earlier in this chapter). The wedding venue may be far from where the groom lives, and so you and the groom have checked into a nearby hotel for the night before. Even if the venue's close by, still make sure that you leave yourselves lots of travelling time.

The groom's wheels

Sitcom characters are the only ones foolish enough to take public transport to their own weddings. And that goes for the best man, too. Can you imagine what a couple of twits you'd look on a delayed train in your wedding outfits? If the groom doesn't want to hire a car, take your own vehicle or – particularly if your wheels are unreliable – hire a taxi. After all, who's going to stop for two worried-looking hitchhikers wearing morning suits? Don't expect the groom to drive. That's your job. He's far too preoccupied to concentrate on the road.

Plan to arrive at the wedding venue at least an hour and a half before all the other guests. You need time to sort out any last minute hiccups and have time to enjoy a premarital drink with all the ushers (see 'Dutch Courage: The Groom's Last Drink as a Free Man' later in this chapter).

The wedding car

Discuss hired transport with the groom and the father of the bride well before the wedding. If the groom hires a special vehicle to whisk him and his wife to the reception, he may ask you to drive him to the ceremony in that car. If the bride and her father arrive at the ceremony in a classy chauffeured vehicle – a Rolls Royce or Bentley is more common than a Capri or Robin Reliant, but each to their own – the married couple may then be driven to the reception in that car after they've got hitched. The bride's father makes his own way to the reception.

If the groom has taken charge of the hire car, accompany him in it to the ceremony and then let him drive his new wife away afterwards.

Band of Brothers: Organising the Ushers

The best place for the ushers to meet up with the groom and best man is at a pub near the wedding venue, where you can all share a premarital drink (see 'Dutch Courage: The Groom's Last Drink as a Free Man' later in this chapter). Distribute the ushers with a copy of the *wedding schedule,* if they don't already have one. This schedule details exactly who, among the wedding party, is expected to do what and when. (See the nearby sidebar 'Sample wedding schedule'.) Ideally, the bride and groom have handed the schedule out to you at the wedding rehearsal (I walk you through the rehearsal in Chapter 4).

Along with the chief usher, you need to quickly run though all the ushers' duties for the ceremony:

✔ **Allocate two ushers to direct the car parking at the wedding venue.** Don't let your own car get boxed in – you need to get to the reception very quickly after the ceremony.

✔ **Place two ushers at the entrance of the wedding venue.** These ushers hand out the *orders of service* to guests and direct them to their seats. Orders of service list the various elements of the wedding service – official words, blessings, vows, hymns, readings, and musical interludes.

✔ **Ask the remaining ushers to stay inside the venue.** They are then on hand to escort elderly or disabled guests to their seats and to ensure that the seats near the front are reserved for the family, bridesmaids and close friends.

As a general rule, the bride's family and guests are on the left and the groom's on the right. The more important the guests, the nearer the front they should sit. (See Chapter 6 for more on seating arrangements.)

✔ **Allocate one usher to give you and the groom the nod just before the bride arrives at the venue door.** A thumbs-up sign should suffice.

✔ **Remind the ushers that they need to help you get the wedding party together for all the photos.** You need all the help you can get for this.

✔ **Allocate one usher to stay behind after the ceremony until everyone has left.** He checks for lost property and picks up stragglers.

✔ **Hand out the buttonholes** (Chapter 4 has more on this floral finery) so that the groom, best man, and ushers are distinguishable by their flowers.

Be a really organised best man and email all the ushers a few days before the wedding to remind them what their duties are. Ideally, you don't want to spring any surprises on them.

Dutch Courage: The Groom's Last Drink as a Free Man

You can hardly expect the groom to get hitched on an empty stomach, can you? A quick drink can allay any last-minute nerves and give him the courage he needs to walk up the aisle.

The prenuptial drink is a key feature of any British wedding day, as traditional now as confetti and speeches. Normally groom, best man and the ushers meet up in the pub nearest the wedding venue about an hour and a half before the ceremony kicks off. This meeting allows the groom to enjoy his final drink as a single man with his closest friends.

Sample wedding schedule

9:00 a.m.: Florist delivers flowers and buttonholes to the bride's mother.

10:00 a.m.: Caterers arrive at bride's house to set up reception

1:00 p.m.: Usher X collects buttonholes from bride's mother.

1.30 p.m.: Groom, best man and all the ushers meet at the Dog and Duck. Buttonholes, and wedding schedules are distributed.

2:00 p.m.: Acme Chauffeurs arrive at bride's house. Groom, best man and all the ushers arrive at the church. Photographer arrives, too.

2.30 p.m.: Acme Chauffeurs drive bride and bride's father to the church. Other guests arrive at the church. Ushers direct the parking and show them to seats.

3:00 p.m.: Wedding!

3:00 p.m.: Band (if the bride and groom have decided to have one) and DJ arrive at bride's house to set up.

3:45 Photographs. (These can take a while.)

4:15 p.m.: Wedding party and guests leave for the reception.

4.45 p.m.: Wedding party lines up to receive guests.

5 p.m. to 7:00 p.m.: Champagne and canapés. Band plays throughout.

7:00 p.m.: Dinner.

8.30 p.m.: Speeches.

9.00 p.m.: Cut the cake.

9.30 p.m.: Dancing.

12.30 a.m.: The wedding couple leave for their hotel.

12.45 a.m.: DJ wraps things up.

1:00 a.m.: Minibuses transport guests to the hotel.

Although slurred vows may elicit a few laughs, the groom has to be in a fit state when he actually ties the knot. So limit his intake to a single pint – or two at a stretch. That's goes for bestie and the ushers, too.

Just before you leave for the wedding venue, ask the groom to hand you the ring. Place the wedding ring safely in your pocket, but don't put it on your own finger. Nerves tend to make the fingers swell, and you don't want any delay when the groom reaches out for the ring during the vows.

Chapter 6

The Actual Ceremony

In This Chapter

▶ Seating the guests

▶ Waiting at the altar

▶ Keeping the ring safe

▶ Signing the paperwork

▶ Helping with the photos

This is it! The moment of truth. Your groom is about to tie the knot, get hitched, take the plunge. And you're at his side, metaphorically holding his hand as he does so.

Your Job's Easy

You just stand next to the groom, provide the ring when requested and let him get on with the ceremony. The groom's job is a lot more psychologically stressful. Keep him cool and reassured, and the ceremony should all run as planned.

- ✔ **1 hour to go:** Groom, best man and all the ushers arrive at the venue.

- ✔ **30 minutes to go:** Early guests start to arrive. Ushers direct the car parking and seat the guests. (See 'Pew! What a Lot of People: Seating the Guests'.)

- ✔ **5 minutes to go:** Bride arrives with her father. Groom and best man stand at the front of the venue.

Ceremony:

✔ Bride and her father walk down the aisle.

✔ Minister or registrar welcomes everyone and commences the order of service.

✔ Readings, poems, prayers and hymns

✔ Minister or registrar asks if there is any reason why the couple should not be wed.

✔ Rings and vows are exchanged.

✔ Minister or registrar marries the couple. 'You may kiss the bride!'

✔ Musical interlude while wedding party signs the register.

✔ Wedding party proceeds back down the aisle and out of the venue. Guests follow.

✔ Photographs are taken by the official photographer in the grounds of the wedding venue.

Pew! What a Lot of People: Seating the Guests

As best man, you're not expected to seat the guests. However, you are expected to greet them as they arrive and oversee any seating congestion that may occur. Once the majority are seated, you then take your position at the right hand of your groom.

At informal weddings, guests can pretty much sit where they like, as long as the front seats are reserved for immediate family and bridesmaids. But at formal weddings, the bride's family and friends sit on the left, and the groom's sit on the right (see Figure 6-1). Ushers ask guests when they arrive which side of the family they're from.

If the father of the bride is paying for the wedding, then chances are a lot more of the guests are on the bride's side than the groom's. The bride's father is probably keen to show off his precious daughter on her special day and may well have his golf buddies and half of his work colleagues in attendance.

Inevitably, the left-hand side of the venue fills up a lot more quickly than the right. I've been to some weddings where the groom's side of the church looked pitifully empty while the bride's side was bulging at the seams. Ushers can avoid this imbalance by sending some of the bride's guests over to the right-hand side.

SEATING PLAN

For a formal wedding here is the traditional seating plan:

LEFT	RIGHT
Bride's parents	Groom and best man
Bride's family and bridesmaids	Groom's parents
Bride's other relatives	Groom's close family
	Groom's other relatives
Bride's friends	Groom's friends
Ushers	Ushers

Figure 6-1: Typical seating plan for a formal wedding.

Nowadays, many couples have been together for years before they get hitched. A lot of their friends are mutual, so where they sit doesn't really matter. Brief the ushers to ask of the guests: 'Bride or groom?' If guests reply 'Both', seat them on the (probably) emptier groom's side.

Remind the ushers to keep the front seats free for the VIPs. Apart from the bride and her father, the last guest to arrive is the mother of the bride. She has pride of place, front left. You don't want her relegated to the back of the venue because the ushers haven't kept a space for her.

At informal weddings, older and more punctual guests can be given priority up front. Young friends of the bride and groom who arrive late won't mind so much if they're stuck at the back or behind a column.

At very formal weddings, ushers may be expected to escort female guests to their seats. But at most ceremonies, unless the guest arrives alone, this act is seen as overly chivalrous. You'd also need a lot of ushers to avoid a bottleneck at the door.

To avoid seating congestion, tell the ushers to fill the venue from near the back of the main seating area. The bridesmaids and close family of the wedding couple always arrive last, and they need to be able to walk straight to their places up front.

Altar-gether Now

You and the groom don't want to be standing for hours, waiting at the altar. Although the groom must be on time (remember, you're responsible for getting the groom at the wedding venue at least one and a half hours before the ceremony), the bride's allowed to be late – and almost inevitably she is. So, as the guests file in, sit down at the front of the venue. Don't feel that you need to stand on ceremony during the entire build-up.

Here comes the bride

Make sure that the ushers at the door give you the nod when the bride's arrival is imminent. A thumbs-up is sufficient. (Check out Chapters 4 and 5 for more on the ushers' duties). Then, you and the groom can take your positions.

This moment is when the nerves can really strike. A groom who's been cool as a cucumber all day may suddenly get the heebie-jeebies as the final seconds tick away. Do whatever you need to do to keep him relaxed. Keep him focused. Keep talking quietly to him. Don't let him panic.

Surviving the service

Some services can be excruciatingly long. I once attended a wedding in France that lasted more than two hours. Here are a few common-sense tips to help you through the ceremony:

- ✔ Don't lock your knees while standing: This action stops the blood flowing to your lower legs and can cause you to fall over.

- ✔ Every few minutes, shift the weight from one leg to the other to keep the blood circulating.

- ✔ Smile. Even if inside you're worried to death.

- ✔ Put your hands by your sides or behind your back, not in your pockets.

- ✔ Don't chew gum. Nail-biting is not a good look.

The old shoe-sole trick

You may feel this little practical joke's a terrible cliché, but the message-on-the-soles-of-the-shoes trick is a classic. This stunt works perfectly if you know that at some point in the ceremony the bride and groom are going to kneel down. Here's what you do:

Just before the groom gets dressed for the wedding, distract him for a moment and grab his shoes. Use white correction fluid to paint 'H E' on the sole of the left shoe and 'L P!' on the sole of the right shoe. Provided that you allow time for the fluid to dry, the groom probably won't notice.

When the time comes for the groom to kneel down at the altar, his back to all the wedding guests, suddenly the message 'HELP!' appears on his shoes. This prank can provide a little light relief.

Just make sure that you get the right letters on the right shoes. 'LP!HE' doesn't have quite the same effect.

Lord of the Ring

The lost ring – the ultimate wedding cliché. Why do so many films and TV programmes feature this scenario, just as the registrar's about to pronounce the couple husband and wife? Probably because this situation happens so easily.

Believe me, you'll have the whole venue laughing at you if you mislay the ring. (Apart from the registrar and the wedding couple, that is, who will want to murder you.) Keeping hold of the ring is your major responsibility throughout the ceremony. Keep the ring safe, in a small jewellery box, in your suit top pocket. If you're really worried, you can always carry a spare dress ring in another pocket for emergencies.

If the bride is giving the groom a ring, too, she normally keeps it on her person and presents hers to the groom when you present the ring the groom bought for her.

Don't put the ring on your own finger for safekeeping. What if you can't get it off quickly? Who's supposed to marry the groom then?

Where the ****'s the groom?

In the old days, if the groom failed to turn up for his own wedding, the best man was expected to make an honest woman of the bride. Best man was like a second in a gentlemen's duel. If his friend couldn't fight, the best man had to take his place.

Fortunately, that tradition is long gone. Unfortunately, if the groom doesn't turn up to get married, your job is to go to find him.

This scenario is not completely unheard of. Last-minute nerves can make a man do many strange things. After months of building himself up to the crucial moment of getting married, he may suddenly lose his bottle.

You have no time to lose. Gather together all the ushers and send out search parties. Don't let the bride or her family know what's going on. If they find out that he's jilted her at the altar, they'll probably want to throttle him.

Check all the obvious places: the pub, the airport, a very high cliff. If you do find him, be prepared for some delicate psychological counselling. He won't have taken the decision to abandon the wedding lightly. A slap around the face and a gruff, 'Pull yourself together, man!' won't improve the situation. At this stage, his thoughts will be focused more on escape than espousal. Emigration to South America may even sound like a good idea.

If you really can't talk him round, you have to tell the bride and her family. Not surprisingly, telling them the bad news will cause tears, much tearing of hair and eventually, extreme anger. The bride's father and brothers will be baying for the groom's blood. In his absence, they may even try to take things out on you.

Don't be surprised. Put yourself in their shoes. The bride has just been jilted at the altar. Maybe thousands of pounds have been spent on the wedding, which now simply isn't going to happen. The whole of the bride's family has been humiliated in front of all their friends.

Whatever you do, don't reveal the whereabouts of the groom. In fact, why not join him on that flight to South America?

Postnuptial Duties

At this stage, bride and groom are wrapped up in each other's wedded bliss. You won't necessarily get sensible answers out of either of them, so the official procedures and the logistics of helping with the photographs are down to you and the ushers.

Registering your approval

Official duties first. To make the wedding legal, the bride and groom must sign the marriage register. In a church, this act is normally done at the very back, behind the altar, or in a separate chamber. At a registry office, the couple sign in front of all the guests.

The bride and groom require two witnesses to sign the register, too – normally they have been asked to participate in this service in advance. Traditionally, the witnesses are two of the four parents, but as best man, your autograph may be required, too. This part is very straightforward. Just follow the instructions.

Marching orders

Proceeding out of the venue to Handel's *Arrival of the Queen of Sheba* is one of the most moving moments of the whole ceremony. Bride and groom obviously go first, followed by best man and bridesmaids. Offer your arm to the chief bridesmaid and remember that dozens of cameras are going to be trained on you. Walk slowly, stand tall and smile. And don't trip up on the bride's train.

Congregate with the wedding party outside the venue, ready for the photographs.

Saying 'Cheese!'

Some wedding photographers find themselves in the awkward situation where they're not quite sure who exactly they should be photographing. Bride and groom are blindingly obvious, but who are the groom's parents? Where's Granny gone? Should Auntie Dot be in the pictures?

Introduce yourself to the photographer while he's setting up. You already have a good idea of where the photographs are to be taken – this point is discussed with the bride and groom at the wedding rehearsal (refer to Chapter 4 for more on what happens at the rehearsal). The photographer expects you to rally together all the various members of the wedding party as and when they're needed. The photographer has a standard list of pictures that he needs to take so ask him for the running order so you know who to get hold of and when. Ask the ushers to help you with this task.

The basic shots needed are

- Bride and groom
- Bride, groom and both sets of parents
- Bride, groom, both sets of parents and bride and groom's siblings
- Bride, groom, best man and chief bridesmaid
- Bride, groom, best man, chief bridesmaid and both sets of parents
- Bride, groom, best man and the ushers
- Bride, groom and all the bridesmaids
- Groom, best man and the ushers
- Bride and all her bridesmaids
- The whole lot (including any grandparents and pageboys)
- Informal pictures

When all the essential shots have been taken, you may find that the bride and groom have commissioned the photographer to snap a few informal pics, with the wedding party laughing and joking.

Guests are always desperate to get to the reception, where the champagne awaits them. You want to get through the photos fairly rapidly so you can free yourself and the ushers for reception duties. But you don't want anyone to be missed out of any of the planned shots. So, rally together the entire wedding party into one big group so that they can step up and have their photos taken quickly when they need to. If family, ushers and bridesmaids are scattered all over the place, the photography session drags on interminably.

Flowers in their hair

Church vicars aren't great fans of confetti, especially if the stuff's not biodegradable. Guests at church weddings know this fact and may hold back from throwing confetti. Check in advance with the vicar. If he agrees on the use of confetti, take the lead and get throwing.

Have several packets of confetti in your pocket and agree with the photographer when to start showering the newly-weds. Provided you time the moment right, confetti always looks great in photos.

Chapter 7

The Wedding Reception

*N*ow for the fun part. The reception is the guests' reward for sitting patiently through the ceremony. By this stage, they're dying for a drink. And, no doubt, so are you. But don't let your hair down too far before you've completed your most important duty of the day: the speech (and if you haven't written it yet, best to check out Chapters 8 and 9, ASAP).

The Reception

Everyone likes to mix things up a little and change the order of the different elements of the reception. For example, many weddings now feature the speeches before, rather than after, the meal. Figure 7-1 shows how the wedding reception normally progresses.

You're by no means the host of the party – that's generally considered the bride and groom or whoever's contributing the most financially toward the event. But as best man, you ought to help get the party moving and grooving. First, you're in charge of getting all the guests to the reception. You can find yourself compèring on the microphone or goading the guests on to the dance floor. You may even have to help deal with guests who've had more to drink than is good for them.

The Reception

* *Arrival of bride, groom, and close family*
* *Arrival of guests*
* *Drinks, often outside venue or in foyer*
* *Receiving line*
* *Meal – and drinks!*
* *Father of bride's speech*
* *Groom's speech*
* *Best man's speech*
* *Toasts*
* *Dancing and socialising*
* *Departure of bride and groom*

Figure 7-1: Order of events at a typical reception.

Guest Appearances

The wedding couple won't be the only people wandering, dazed, out of the ceremony. A lot of the guests, especially close family, have had their emotions stretched by the day's events.

If the trip to the reception venue is at all complicated, you can guarantee that you're going to get stragglers. The best man and his ushers have to marshal everyone from the ceremony to the reception. The newly-weds depart for the reception in their own vehicle. The other guests may well have directions to the reception venue on their wedding invitations, but they're still going to expect logistical help from you.

Keep things simple. Appoint one usher to stay at the ceremony venue until everyone has left. He can also collect any mislaid hats, presents or bridesmaids. As everyone mills around outside, you need to make a loud announcement – to get their full attention – and explain how to get to the reception.

The easiest weddings are those where the reception is within walking distance of the ceremony. Sod's law says that the nuptials you're best man for has the two venues miles apart.

If the route is difficult and you have enough ushers, you can post an usher at all the major junctions along the route. Standing by the road in their morning suits with bright buttonholes, the ushers can be far more effective than signposts. Try to encourage the guests to leave the ceremony all at the same time. If they travel in a huge convoy, they're less likely to get lost.

You, meanwhile, have to get to the reception, sharpish. You need to be there to help with any last-minute preparations, or in case of problems with the band, or the DJ or the caterers. Whatever may happen, you can always lend a helping hand.

For What We Are About to Receive

The receiving line is becoming less fashionable these days, but some more formal weddings still have one – in which case you may be required to be included.

Here's what happens: The newly-weds and both sets of parents line up to greet all the guests officially. Traditionally, the order of the receiving line is like this:

1. The bride's mother and father

2. The groom's parents

3. The newly-weds

4. The best man and the chief bridesmaid (including these two is at the bride and groom's discretion, but if you are in the line, then you stand at the very end).

The line always causes a bottleneck, as all the guests congratulate the wedding party and introduce themselves to the side of the family they haven't met yet. The affair can seem a bit like when the Queen inspects her troops – and often just as contrived.

Master of All He Surveys

Life can be so unfair. Not only are you expected to deliver a scintillating speech (check out Chapters 8 and 9), but the couple may ask you to be *master of ceremonies (MC)* to boot.

At formal weddings, a *toastmaster* may be appointed to MC before and between speeches. At small, less formal affairs, this responsibility often falls to the best man.

Here's what you need to do:

- ✔ Announce dinner when served.
- ✔ Check that the microphone for the speeches is working properly.
- ✔ Introduce the father of the bride before he makes the first speech.

In the absence of a huge gong, you're going to need something of a bellow when the time comes to announcing dinner. Tell everyone to check the arrangements on the seating plan and then just let them tuck into the wine.

Traditionally, the speeches take place after dessert, but a lot of couples now stage them at the beginning of, or even before, the meal. If any of the speakers is nervous (fumble over to the section on nerves in Chapter 9 for more information), this spares them the discomfort of having to sit through the entire dinner, worrying about the impending speech.

Once you and the other speakers are ready for your moment of fame, stand up and jangle a spoon loudly in a glass. Everyone can take this to be the signal for the start of the speeches. As MC, you introduce the first speaker – normally the bride's father. Once he's finished, he then introduces the groom, who in turn introduces you.

Being the host with the most

Technically, the best man is not the wedding host. But the newly-weds always appreciate a bit of help on this front. With perhaps hundreds of guests to organise, they're going to need all hands on deck. Otherwise, the ship's likely to sink.

Is top table top priority?

Traditionally, the top table features bride, groom, best man, chief bridesmaid and both sets of parents. If the table has room, ushers and other bridesmaids may join them, too.

The problem with this setup is that best man, ushers and bridesmaids are separated from their partners. Step-parents also complicate matters. For this reason, a lot of wedding couples are now doing away with the top table entirely.

If you think about the setup, this makes a lot of sense. Why should bride and groom sit next to their in-laws? They will have plenty of time for that over the next 30 Christmases. Instead, the couple may share a table with best man and his partner, chief bridesmaid and her partner and a few close friends and their partners. The reception meal should be as enjoyable as possible for the newly-weds. Besides, the parents-in-law can have more fun sat with their own friends.

You need to keep focused for the after-dinner speech. A couple of glasses of champagne can ease your nerves and lubricate your larynx. But any more than that and you risk slurring your delivery. Wait until after your speech before you hit the bottle.

Take your partner by the hand

The newly-weds' first dance is sacrosanct. They may have been planning the song and their moves for months. And they should be allowed to enjoy the moment alone on the dance floor.

However, about three-quarters of the way through, they'll have had enough of the spotlight and be wondering where the guests are.

People inevitably hold back from joining them for fear of interrupting something special. Therefore, you must take the lead. Agree with bride and groom beforehand at which juncture you can join them on the dance floor. Then, grab your partner or the chief bridesmaid and set an example. Once you start strutting your stuff, everyone else realises the time's right to join in.

Wedding winos

Bestie is hardly expected to be a bouncer. But if things get a bit rowdy, you can certainly help calm things down. The wine can be flowing all night long, and you may find a few guests who've had one too many – or ten too many, in some cases.

Emotions are high at weddings. With so many family members all in one room, tempers are inevitably going to get a little frayed.

You should keep an eye out for any potential rucks before they happen.

If any of the guests looks a little worse for wear, try to get them away from the reception and as far away as possible from the bar.

Don't just haul them out by the scruff of the neck. Use a little diplomacy. One idea is to tell them that they have a phone call for them in the main house or at the hotel reception. When you've got them away from the party, you can ply them with coffee and get them to sober up.

Seeing Off the Newly-weds

In the old days, so keen were bride and groom to consummate their marriage that they'd rush off to their honeymoon halfway through the reception, leaving the guests to carry on the party without them. Nowadays, the couple is positively expected to be the life and soul of the reception – the bride and groom can quite literally dance until dawn. Sometimes, especially at marquee weddings, the couple may even host a family lunch the next day.

The best man is there to ease the couple's transition into married life by, for example:

- ✔ Helping them pack the car.

- ✔ Taking charge of any clothing that the groom hired.

- ✔ Ensuring that the wedding presents end up in the right place.

Engulfed as they surely are in nuptial bliss, bride and groom will be in no position to remember such details.

Kippers and tin cans

Decorating the car is another one of those traditional rituals that's become a wedding cliché. But this ritual is an important cliché. Whatever you do, don't pass up the chance to tie tin cans to the back bumper or spray 'Just Married!' across the rear windscreen. Balloons and streamers can add to the effect.

Rotten kippers in the engine may be stretching things a bit though.

The couple can revel in all the attention they get from other motorists as they drive away with cans rattling and streamers billowing in the wind. And the photos will look great.

You may be tempted to really monkey about with the newly-weds' car. But don't take your pranks too far. Remember that they may have a plane to catch. Stuck on the motorway en route to the airport isn't much of a honeymoon.

Part III
The Speech

Top Five Subjects to Avoid in Your Speech

✔ No one, least of all the bride, is under any false impressions about the groom's innocence when you come to his past loves. But you don't need to bring up the subject of **ex-girlfriends** on the wedding day.

✔ These days, at least one-half of the wedding couple may be a divorcé(e). And if that's the case, at least half of your audience members knows about this fact. They probably even attended the first wedding. But now is not the time to remind them of their **ex-wife.**

✔ He may have had the clap, but no one's going to applaud you for telling them about his **STDs.**

✔ **Drinking and gambling** are all for the stag party – and the stag party only.

✔ **Racist, homophobic and mother-in-law jokes are** so passé. You're the best man, not Bernard Manning.

Find out all you need to know about public speaking at www. dummies.com/extras/beingthebestmanuk.

In this part . . .

- ✔ Find great quotes and anecdotes to make your speech one to remember.

- ✔ Become a polished public speaker so that no one really knows how nervous you are.

- ✔ Know what details and anecdotes to put in your speech – and what to leave out.

- ✔ Discover how to practice so that your delivery is smooth as button and you don't go on so long that you've lost half your audience.

- ✔ Find out how to project your voice so that even those at the back of the room can hear you.

Chapter 8

Writing the Speech

. . . .

In This Chapter

▶ Selecting a speech format

▶ Writing out your speech

▶ Choosing the opening line

▶ Deciding what to include – and what not to include

. . . .

*Y*ou're bound to procrastinate with the speech. Everyone does. Some best men even put off writing their piece until the night before the wedding. But they tend to be the best men who give the weakest speeches.

Don't leave writing the speech until the last minute. Start at least a couple of months before the wedding day, well before you get caught up in all the preparations for the stag do and the wedding itself.

The key to a great speech is preparation. Don't, whatever you do, assume that you can just wing the speech on the day. You're going to be up in front of possibly hundreds of people and they're expecting you to make them laugh. Or at least chuckle. The bride and groom have pinned their hopes on you – this is, after all, one of your key tasks as best man. You're the main act, so make sure that you give your audience value for money.

Even the world's best orators spend precious hours writing and practising their chosen words. The bad news is that you've got to do the same thing. The good news is that the more you practise, the easier the ordeal gets.

Structuring Your Speech

A best man's speech that follows the traditional format to the very letter can sound a bit stilted. Be flexible and give your speech the personal touch, depending on how formal the wedding is. But make sure that you don't leave out any key elements. Just as in pantomimes, a best man's speech has certain conventional milestones where the guests know that they're expected to laugh, cheer and boo. Include these in your own speech and get everyone on your side. Follow this guide, and you can get in everything you need:

1. **Deliver a killer opening line.**

   A crucial point is to get the guests with you right from the start. An original opening line that raises a laugh or a cheer can achieve this (the section 'Kicking Off on a Good Note' later in this chapter can help you).

2. **Thank the other speakers.**

   The best man's speech almost always comes last, so you must thank the groom, the father of the bride and any other speakers for their speeches (see 'Acknowledging the other speakers' later in this chapter).

3. **Unsettle the groom.**

   Everyone knows that your job's to assassinate the groom's character. So why not drop in a little teaser about all the embarrassing things you're about to reveal? You can keep him on his toes and give the guests something to look forward to.

4. **Thank the newly-weds on behalf of the bridesmaids.**

   Thanking the bride and groom for the presents they gave the bridesmaids traditionally is your most important speech duty. So don't leave this part out! (Check out 'Replying on behalf of the bridesmaids' later in this chapter.)

5. **Congratulate the wedding couple.**

   By this stage, the couple have received congratulations from everyone in the room. Several times. But you've still got to include these best wishes in your speech (help is at hand in 'Congratulating the happy couple' later in this chapter).

6. **Admire the bride.**

   The bride has personal compliments coming out of her ears. But if you add your own compliments, you're sure to get a cheer (see 'Complimenting the gorgeous bride' later in this chapter).

7. **Ridicule the groom.**

   Having told everyone how wonderful his wife is, you now have the perfect opportunity to lampoon the groom. Here's your chance to really get the guests laughing. You need to include some hilarious stories about what a twit the groom often is (check out 'Dishing the Dirt on the Groom' later in this chapter). Be merciless, but don't humiliate him (see 'Don't mention the war: Subjects to avoid' later in this chapter).

8. **Get serious.**

   Yes, you've got to make the people laugh. But you've got to include some emotional stuff, too. You're not just a stand-up comedian. You need to add some heartfelt and poignant stuff about what a brilliant bloke the groom really is and what a close friend he's been to you over the years. Remember to say how lucky the groom is and what a great couple they make.

9. **Read messages from absentees.**

   If the real messages are a bit pedestrian, then you can always make up a few spurious ones – as long as the guests realise they're gags.

10. **Quote a few famous lines or a poem.**

    Choose the appropriate words, and they can imbue your speech with a bit of gravity. And by this stage, you'll probably need some. ('Quote me on that' later in this chapter offers some suggestions.)

11. **Propose a toast.**

    The toast is a signal to the guests that the speech is over. This point in time is also a chance for them to take a slug of champagne (drink your way through 'Raise your glasses' later in this chapter).

Putting Pen to Paper

Disciplining yourself to sit down and start writing your speech can be the hardest part. Worry not. Once you get going, things soon move along.

If you're used to writing on a computer, proceed just like that. If you're more comfortable scribbling things on paper, then that's fine, too. You can always type your scribbles up later.

Start off by listing the key bullet points. Use the list in 'Structuring Your Speech' earlier in this chapter as a guide. As you get the ingredients clear in your mind, you can gradually flesh them out with full sentences and anecdotes.

Provided that you know the groom very well – and you should, since you're his best man – the speech probably won't take that long to write. Sorting out the basic structure should be an evening's work. Then over the next few weeks, as you go on the stag do and prepare for the wedding, you can add to the material, update it and flesh it out until you have the final version. A couple of nights before the big day, you can give your speech the final touches.

Does length matter?

Speech length depends on how formal the wedding is. The normal running length is between 10 and 15 minutes. If a member of the Royal Family asked you to be his best man, you'd probably regale the guests at Buckingham Palace for a bit longer. If the reception includes just close family and friends in a restaurant, then you're likely to want to keep your speech short and sweet.

Always check in advance with the groom and the bride's father how long their speeches are likely to be. Yours should always be the longest, but not by miles. The guests want to laugh, not yawn.

Going to press

No one's expecting you to memorise your speech and deliver it like a politician on Election Day. You're going to need notes or a hard copy of the speech itself. Mind you, if you *can* memorise it, you'll impress the pants off everyone there.

How much you commit to memory all depends on your confidence and style. The best speakers tend to partly memorise their speech and use cue cards with bullet points written on them as an aide-memoire (I talk about this a bit more in Chapter 9).

If you're worried you're going to forget huge chunks of the speech, print the entire thing on to small sheets of paper. Don't use A4 or larger: If you get nervous, the paper shakes in your hands, and you can look very unprofessional. Ideally, use small pieces of card, like those in card indexes.

Unless you're very confident that you know exactly what you're doing, don't get too ambitious by using overhead projectors or computer presentations. The technology's bound to let you down. Besides, this is a best man's speech, not a lecture.

Kicking Off on a Good Note

Like a stand-up comic, you need to get your audience on side from the very start. And this means that you need a killer first line. The line doesn't need to be hilarious or completely original (none of the ones listed here are), but a cliché or a private joke isn't going to work.

Try to give the guests something that they can laugh or cheer at. They'll be primed and up for this moment, so even just a little witticism or a quick remark about what a superb time everyone's having can suffice. Obviously, the funnier you make your opening line, the better. But try not to make this line sound stilted or false.

Here are some examples of great openings:

> ✔ You may not be aware of this, but I've actually congratulated the groom already. 'Well done!' I told him. 'You'll always look back on this day as the happiest and most noble thing you've ever done, your greatest achievement, your finest hour.' Fitting words, I think you'll agree, at the end of a fantastic stag do.

✔ In the run-up to the wedding, like many couples, [bride] and [groom] had a few problems sorting out the seating plans. They kept arguing about who should sit where. As best man, I decided to step in and help them figure it out. In the end, we decided to use the wedding gift list as a guide: Those of you who bought the most expensive items would sit nearest the front, and then we'd continue back from there, in decreasing order of generosity. [*Raising voice*] So if you can hear me at the back, on behalf of [bride] and [groom], thank you very much for the tin opener!

✔ The first time I ever met [groom], I was impressed by his taste in clothing, his sartorial elegance. Stylish, debonair, cool – he had all the clothes a young man could possibly require. It wasn't long before I started emulating his dress sense. He and I used to go out on the town together, dolled up to the nines, both of us kitted out in the same style. It was all great until one day my mother found out that I'd been pinching clothes from her wardrobe.

✔ You've got no idea how much I was looking forward to today. After all the time I've been friends with [groom], he has at long last admitted that I am in fact the best man.

✔ I've been told that a best man has three essential duties:

1. He must help the groom get dressed on the morning of his big day. Well, I've got to say, he really should know how to do that himself by now.

2. He must make sure that the groom relieves himself just before the wedding ceremony. Well, I can tell you, I don't mind packing him off to the loo, but I point blank refuse to actually check he's done the business.

3. He must check the groom's face and hair are in order. Unfortunately, if God couldn't get it right the first time, then I haven't got a hope in hell.

✔ Making the best man's speech is a bit like having sex with the Queen. It's a great honour to be asked, but, let's be honest, no one really wants to do it.

✔ Sod's law. The first time [groom]'s ever paid for my food, and I was so nervous about my speech that I couldn't even eat a mouthful.

✔ You'll be relieved to learn that just before my speech, [bride] gave me some strict instructions on subjects I wasn't allowed to mention. [*Remove a big stack of cue cards from your pocket and dump them on the floor behind you*] That's that sorted then. Happy now, [bride]?

✔ Unaccustomed as I am to pubic spanking . . . Oops!

✔ You may have noticed a little bit of gambling going on behind the scenes. Well, apparently, there's a bet on how long my speech is going to be. In fact, I couldn't resist having a bit of a flutter myself. My estimate was a good hour and three-quarters. With the kitty currently standing at around 250 quid, you may as well relax, get comfortable and prepare yourselves for a very long afternoon indeed.

✔ Watching [bride's father] and [groom] speaking before me, I was suddenly struck by how much they have in common. Do you realise? It's the first time in 30 years that [bride's father] has been able to talk for more than 3 minutes without being contradicted by his wife. And it's the last time in 30 years that [groom] will do the very same thing.

✔ [Groom] and I are very close. Over the years I've been like a mother to him. I've seen him crawl round the house in his birthday suit. I've watched him drink from the bottle. I've had to dress him. I've had to clean up all his mess. I've even had to teach him how to walk.

✔ Fret not, ladies and gentlemen. My speech is going to last only a couple of minutes. That's because of my throat. If I carry on too long, [bride] says she'll throttle it.

✔ People in the wedding party always tend to get a bit nervous on occasions like this. Spare a thought for [bride]. She's just realised who she's now married to.

✔ When [groom] asked me to be his best man, I told him I was honoured, but that he was really better off asking someone else. He insisted and offered me £100 for my troubles. I must say I was very angry with him for thinking that I could be bribed. He then offered me £200. Again I refused. We carried on like this for quite a while. Anyway, good afternoon, ladies and gentlemen. I can't tell you what an honour it is to be [groom]'s best man.

Including the Essentials

Don't get too obsessed about making your speech funny.
Well-placed jokes are crucial. But a lot of your speech can be
taken up with certain key elements that you mustn't forget to
include.

Acknowledging the other speakers

Since your speech is almost always the final one of the day,
you need to turn to the groom and bride's father and thank
them for their own speeches out of courtesy. They may have
bored you all rigid, but you've still got to sound grateful for
their scintillating words.

In a way, the other speakers are the warm-up acts for you –
the main show. You would sound churlish not to acknowledge
them kindly.

Replying on behalf of the bridesmaids

Most newly-weds present their bridesmaids and pageboys
with gifts to thank them for their help in getting them down
the aisle. Since the bridesmaids almost never get the chance
to deliver speeches and the pageboys aren't tall enough to
reach the microphone, part of your role is to thank the bride
and groom for these presents.

You can also take this chance to reiterate how beautiful the
bridesmaids look. And don't worry about whether this fact
is really true. Some of the bridesmaids may not exactly be
oil paintings, but that's not for you to judge. As far as you're
concerned, they're all beauties, and you're just dying to wax
lyrical about them.

Congratulating the happy couple

On many occasions during your speech, you may find that
you risk sounding too cheesy. The trick is to use earnest
heartfelt words. Avoid anything too slushy or schmaltzy. You

don't want the guests using the champagne chillers as sick buckets.

However, you mustn't leave out the necessary congratulations for the newly-weds. Look at them with sincerity as you wish them all the best. Tell them how proud you are to be their best man.

If you start hearing too many 'aaahs' from your audience, you can always counter the compliment with something a bit more sarcastic:

- ✔ Those of you who now need sick buckets, they're just outside the marquee entrance.

- ✔ [Bride], make sure that you always treat him just like a little puppy – lots of exercise, plenty of affection, three meals a day and a loose lead.

- ✔ [Bride and groom] really have it all. Individually, they were both very successful. Together, they can accomplish anything. There's just no stopping them now. Unless, of course, [groom]'s court hearing goes the wrong way.

Complimenting the gorgeous bride

In their eagerness to rabbit on about the groom, a lot of best men forget to incorporate the bride into their speeches. Admittedly, she has been complimented no end by her new husband and most of the guests, but this fact doesn't mean that no room's left for a bit more flattery from you.

Admiring the bride is also a great way to rouse the crowd if your speech seems to be flagging. Just mention how beautiful she looks, what a catch she is and how fortunate the groom is to have found her. Suddenly your audience awakens from their slumbers and injects some life back into your speech with some loud clapping and cheering.

Dishing the Dirt on the Groom

This part is the bit they've all been waiting for. Time for a bit of character assassination. But don't be tempted to take things too far. The groom won't mind everyone laughing at his expense, but you shouldn't reveal anything he can't brush aside after the speech. Some things are just too close to the bone – so don't avoid reading 'Don't mention the war: Subjects to avoid' later in this chapter. Keep the humour mischievous, not cruel.

Character traits

Every groom has some funny characteristic or quirk. As long as this point is something that everyone can appreciate, you're sure to get a laugh. Avoid obscure references and in jokes. You want the older guests who don't know him that well to see the funny side, too. Here are a few ideas:

- **If the groom is a bad cook:** When I used to share a flat with [groom], he had the job of cooking all the meals. I had the job of going from room to room, taking out the batteries from the smoke alarms.

- **If the groom is lazy:** [Groom] is a very lucky man. His job lets him work 8 hours and sleep 8 hours. The only problem is that they're always the same 8 hours.

- **If the groom has a rotten taste in music:** I promised [groom] I wouldn't reveal what his favourite band was as a kid. But later on, if anyone wants to Take A Chance on Me, just Gimme! Gimme! Gimme! a few drinks or some Money, Money, Money, and, Knowing Me, Knowing You, I might just let it slip.

- **If the groom is a bad singer:** I'd like to say that [groom] sings with lots of feeling. But let's be honest: If he had any true feelings, he wouldn't sing at all.

- **If the groom is slightly dim:** In all the years I've known [groom], no one has ever questioned his intellectual ability. In fact, come to think of it, I don't think anyone has ever even mentioned it.

- **If the groom is talkative:** [Groom] has the uncanny ability to talk for hours on any subject . . . and days if he actually knows anything about it.

- **If the groom is unfit:** [Groom] always makes sure that he gets loads of exercise. Just the other week he was out five nights running.

> ✔ **If the groom is bald:** [Bride] asked [groom] and me to pay a quick visit to the hairdresser yesterday. Me for a haircut and [groom] just for a chat.

Anecdotes and ideas

Most best men have known their grooms for years, even decades. Think for a while about all the times you've spent together, and you'll soon unearth plenty of material you can use to compose witty anecdotes.

Remember when you first met each other? Maybe you were at school or university together or perhaps you both worked in the same office. Even if you haven't known him that long, you may have played sport or wasted many valuable hours down the pub together. All of these escapades can give you lots of material to work into your speech.

The groom's close friends and siblings are sure to have lots of funny stories about his younger days. Email or phone them and ask them to jot down some ideas. Then choose the ones that potentially sound the funniest and get the person who offered them to dish the dirt. Examples of this sort of material may include

- ✔ What he was like as a kid
- ✔ His first car
- ✔ Previous jobs
- ✔ Family holidays
- ✔ Pets
- ✔ Nicknames
- ✔ Childhood habits
- ✔ Strange hobbies

You can dig up an endless amount of material – some will be highly embarrassing. All you need to do is ask the right person.

Why not ask the groom's parents whether they have some of his old school reports kicking about? Perhaps his relatives have kept some cards he wrote when he was a kid. Friends from school or university may even have copies of bad essays that he wrote.

Don't let the facts get in the way of a good story. If you need to elaborate or exaggerate to make the story funnier, that's fine. Try to draw the line at complete fabrication, though.

Don't mention the war: Subjects to avoid

Your job is to make the groom squirm. By all means use your jokes and anecdotes to embarrass him – that's par for the course. But avoid humiliating him. His family and in-laws are among your audience, and they don't need (and probably don't want) to know about some of his past secrets. If in doubt, leave it out. Here are some big no-nos:

- ✔ **Ex-girlfriends:** No one, least of all the bride, is under any false impressions about the groom's innocence when you come to his past loves. But you don't need to bring up the subject on the wedding day.

- ✔ **Ex-wives:** These days, at least one half of the wedding couple may be a divorce(e). And if that's the case, at least half of your audience knows about this fact. They probably even attended the first wedding. But now is not the time to remind them.

- ✔ **STDs:** He may have had the clap, but no one's going to applaud you for telling them.

- ✔ **Drink, drugs and gambling:** That's all for the stag party – and the stag party only.

- ✔ **Racist, homophobic and mother-in-law jokes:** They're so passé. You're the best man, not Bernard Manning.

- ✔ **Adult jokes:** Seaside postcard humour is fine, but graphic nun-and-vicar jokes may offend the older guests and confuse the pageboys.

Whatever you do, absolutely do not take the mickey out of any of the following:

- The bride
- The bride's parents
- The bridesmaids
- The wedding ceremony
- The reception

Most brides have spent a long time dolling themselves up and splashed a lot of cash to celebrate the big day. Your joke's going to sound wrong no matter how clever you think the wording is.

 Knowing how far you can take the rude jokes and sexual innuendoes is a tricky one. The older guests may be a bit old-fashioned, but they probably won't be prudish. You can bet your life that they were exchanging smutty jokes before you were born. However, that doesn't mean you can turn the air blue or regale everyone with graphic tales of the groom's sexual exploits. Subtle innuendo is often funnier and far more sophisticated than out-and-out filth. Err on the side of caution.

Safe targets

When you come to think of the groom, you always find great scope for ridicule. All you need is a bit of imagination. You can start off with his appearance – is he short, tall, over-weight, bald, myopic? Has he got a dodgy haircut? Does he dress badly? Is he scruffy?

Then move on to his character ('Character traits' earlier in this chapter can give you a few ideas). Hobbies are always worth a bit of mileage, as are manners, dress sense, and skills in the kitchen. The groom's ability (or lack of) on the sports field is sure to raise a few laughs. And once you start analysing his personality, you find no end of joke material.

Absent Without Leave

You always get a few invited guests who can't make the wedding, whether a cousin in Australia or a bed-ridden auntie with just a few marbles rolling round in her head. In the run-up to the wedding day, you need to check with the bride and the mother of the bride whether any guests unable to come have sent messages of congratulations.

Traditionally, absent guests used to send such messages by telegram. Nowadays, you probably get a few cards and some emails. When you read them, give them the necessary gravitas they deserve. At the end, you can read out a couple of joke messages to get a laugh. Here's an example:

> *This one's from [groom]'s football team, none of whom could make it today because they're playing in their league cup final. They sent the following message of congratulations: 'In our experience, [groom] has been absolutely useless in every position. We hope [bride] has more luck!'*

Quote Me on That

Quotations and poems are generally a sign that you're coming to the end of your speech. You don't *have* to wait this long – you can put them right at the front if you want to. But because they're supposed to summarise the groom's character, or encapsulate his relationship with his new wife or even encapsulate your relationship as one of his best friends, they're more sensibly placed at the end.

Do your guests a favour. Don't use anything overly sentimental and keep the quotations or poems short. Yours is, after all, the third speech of the day. The overall running time of the three speeches may already be as much as 45 minutes. (The total time shouldn't come to that though – ideally, just over 20 minutes is adequate, as I mention earlier in this chapter in 'Does length matter?'). You're sure to have regaled your audience wonderfully, so they won't be bored. But they may be dying for the loo.

Some great quotes

> *I pay very little regard . . . to what a young person says on the subject of marriage. If they profess a disinclination for it, I only set it down that they haven't seen the right person yet.*

> Jane Austen

A good marriage is one which allows for change and growth in the individuals and in the way they express their love.

Pearl Buck

A princely marriage is the brilliant edition of a universal fact, and as such it rivets mankind.

Walter Bagehot

We are all born for love. It is the principle of existence, and its only end.

Benjamin Disraeli

In love the paradox occurs that two beings become one and yet remain two.

Erich Fromm

Marriage is the union of disparate elements. Male and female. Yin and yang. Proton and electron. What are we talking about here? Nothing less than the very tension that binds the universe. You see, when we look at marriage, people, we're looking at creation itself. 'I am the sky,' says the Hindu bridegroom to the bride. 'You are the earth. We are sky and earth united . . . You are my husband. You are my wife. My feet shall run because of you. My feet shall dance because of you. My heart shall beat because of you. My eyes see because of you. My mind thinks because of you and I shall love because of you.'

Diane Frolov and Andrew Schneider, Northern Exposure

The more you invest in a marriage, the more valuable it becomes.

Amy Grant

A good marriage is like a good trade: Each thinks he got the better deal.

Ivern

The meeting of two personalities is like the contact of two chemical substances: If there is any reaction, both are transformed.

Carl Jung

Love is everything it's cracked up to be. . . . It really is worth fighting for, being brave for, risking everything for.

Erica Jong

The moment you have in your heart this extraordinary thing called love and feel the depth, the delight, the ecstasy of it, you will discover that for you the world is transformed.

J. Krishnamurti

All married couples should learn the art of battle as they should learn the art of making love. Good battle is objective and honest – never vicious or cruel. Good battle is healthy and constructive, and brings to a marriage the principle of equal partnership.

Ann Landers

A successful marriage requires falling in love many times, always with the same person.

Mignon McLaughlin

A successful marriage is an edifice that must be rebuilt every day.

Andre Maurois

Age does not protect you from love. But love, to some extent, protects you from age.

Jeanne Moreau

Marriage – as its veterans know well – is the continuous process of getting used to things you hadn't expected.

Tom Mullen

After seven years of marriage, I'm sure of two things – first, never wallpaper together, and second, you'll need two bathrooms . . . both for her. The rest is a mystery, but a mystery I love to be involved in.

Dennis Miller

An occasional lucky guess as to what makes a wife tick is the best a man can hope for. Even then, no sooner has he learned how to cope with the tick than she tocks.

Ogden Nash

'Marriage'. This I call the will that moves two to create the one which is more than those who created it.

Friedrich Nietzsche

Intimacy is what makes a marriage. Not a ceremony, not a piece of paper from the state.

Kathleen Norris

Never marry but for love; but see that thou lovest what is lovely.

William Penn

Marriage is the highest state of friendship. If happy it lessens our cares by dividing them, at the same time that it doubles our pleasures by mutual participation.

Samuel Richardson

For one human being to love another; that is perhaps the most difficult of all our tasks, the ultimate, the last test and proof, the work for which all other work is but preparation.

Rainer Maria Rilke

I love being married. It's so great to find that one special person you want to annoy for the rest of your life.

Rita Rudner

One word frees us of all the weight and pain of life: That word is 'love'.

Sophocles

To love deeply in one direction makes us more loving in all others.

Anne-Sophie Swetchine

Chains do not hold a marriage together. It is threads, hundreds of tiny threads which sew people together through the years. That is what makes a marriage last – more than passion or even sex!

Simone Signoret

I would say that the surest measure of a man's or a woman's maturity is the harmony, style, joy, and dignity he creates in his marriage, and the pleasure and inspiration he provides for his spouse.

Benjamin Spock

That is what marriage really means: helping one another to reach the full status of being persons, responsible and autonomous beings who do not run away from life.

Paul Tournier

To love and be loved is to feel the sun from both sides.

David Viscott

In marriage, each partner is to be an encourager rather than a critic, a forgiver rather than a collector of hurts, an enabler rather than a reformer.

H. Norman Wright and Gary J. Oliver

All love that has not friendship for its base, is like a mansion built upon sand.

Ella Wheeler Wilcox

Poetry in motion

When you come to choosing an appropriate poem, you're going to have to do a bit of research. You may have a favourite verse that you think sums up the newly-weds. Or the groom may have told you about a poem close to their hearts.

Websites can be useful, although most of the material out there tends to be overly sentimental. Try some of the following:

- ✔ www.hitched.co.uk
- ✔ www.poemhunter.com
- ✔ www.youandyourwedding.co.uk
- ✔ www.poemsource.com
- ✔ www.lovepoemsandquotes.com
- ✔ www.poemsforfree.com
- ✔ www.poets.org

If you're feeling really adventurous, why not pen a poem yourself? Your poem may not be quite up to the level of the professionals, but your thoughts can sound a lot more meaningful. And the bride and groom will appreciate your efforts.

For a really special poem, you can use a company that writes personalised poems. Generally, you supply the company with a list of facts and anecdotes about the groom and/or bride and they compose a personalised rhyme for your speech. You have to pay, of course. Try these:

- ✔ www.theweddingpoet.co.uk

- ✔ www.poemwriter.co.uk

- ✔ www.apoemforyou.co.uk

- ✔ www.bignosepoetry.com

- ✔ www.poemfactory.com

Raise your glasses

However unorthodox your speech, you must bring your words to a close with a toast to the bride and groom. Don't spring the toast on your audience – give them a few moments' notice so that they can fill their glasses and get ready to stand up.

The toast is an obvious end point to your speech. Always finish off with a simple energetic phrase that everyone in the room can bellow together and clink their glasses to – something like 'To the bride and groom!' or 'To the happy couple!' Just as your opening line should energise your audience, so should your closing line.

Here are a few toasts you may like to use:

> *To the bride and groom. May their marriage be long and always happy. May their children be as beautiful as they are. And may every wedding speech they listen to be shorter and funnier than mine.*

> *And now I come to the one part of my speech that isn't a duty. On behalf of everyone here, may I wish you both eternal happiness and a long and fruitful marriage.*

> *Here's to you. Here's to your future. Here's to the best thing you both ever did.*

My greatest wish is that your love should grow so deeply that in years to come you will look back upon this day as the day you loved one another the least.

May the roof above your heads never fall in. And may you both never fall out.

May 'for better or worse' be far better than worse.

A toast to the beautiful bride. A toast to the fortunate groom. A toast to the person that tied. A toast to all in the room.

May the best day of your past be the worst day of your future.

Chapter 9

Delivering and Presenting Your Speech

*T*he way in which you present yourself in front of your audience and deliver your words is just as important as the actual content of your speech – maybe more so. Your stance and the projection of your voice can make the difference between a great speech and a mediocre drone. Engaging your audience is crucial.

Just look at the professionals. Next time you're watching TV, notice how politicians, presenters and newsreaders communicate with their viewers. They've all got stage presence. They all use body language, eye contact, varying pitch and tone and enunciation to get their message across.

Most of them weren't born with any more stage presence than you or me. Nearly all of them have been trained by their employers to improve their public speaking. As best man, you can also benefit from a bit of training. The difference is you don't need an employer to send you on a course. Just follow a few common-sense tips.

Practise Makes Perfect

You don't think that David Cameron or Jack Dee just stand up and deliver their words without practising them beforehand do you? And they're professionals. We mere mortals need to rehearse our speeches even more.

About two weeks before the wedding, you need to have a near-enough final version of your speech committed to paper (check out Chapter 8 for more on the content of the speech). You can make little amendments in the final run-up to the big day, but by now you should have something pretty close to the actual words you intend to deliver.

Keep a copy of the speech with you at all times. Use any chance you get to read through the speech out loud.

You've been framed

If you haven't got a camcorder of your own, try to borrow one. Record yourself making your speech. While playing the recording back, make notes on how you do. Focus on:

- ✔ **Stance:** Do you look comfortable? Is your body language friendly and positive? Keep hands out of pockets and avoid moving around too much. Keep looking up at the guests in between sentences.

- ✔ **Pace:** Aim to slow your speech down as much as you can. The variety of pace keeps your audience listening.

- ✔ **Enunciation:** Really articulate your mouth so that your words are projected to the back of the room.

Try to improve in all these areas each time you re-record your speech.

You'll likely be amazed how each subsequent recording makes your words sound smoother and your delivery much more confident.

If you can't get hold of a camcorder, use alternative techno-logical aids. Virtually all cameras and mobile phones have video facilities nowadays. Simply prop it up on a table and start filming yourself.

Mirror, mirror on the wall

Reciting your speech to a mirror can be surprisingly effective. Try to use a full-length mirror so that you can observe your stance and body language as you speak. If possible, stand about 10 feet away. This way trains you to keep looking up at your audience – which is crucial to engaging your listeners.

Some friendly advice

If you want a friend to give you a second opinion on your speech, that friend needs to fulfil three criteria. He should be

- ✔ Honest
- ✔ Not a friend of the bride or the groom
- ✔ Not invited to the wedding

That way, he can give you constructive and impartial feedback, and he's able to spot anything inappropriate that may have slipped into your speech. Also, you don't risk revealing your best jokes before the big day.

Any time, any place, anywhere

Keep a copy of your speech on you at all times. You're like an actor learning lines: Whenever you've got a spare few minutes, read through your words and gradually you commit them to memory. Memorising them makes things a lot easier if you decide to use bullet points and cue cards rather than reading out the whole speech verbatim.

A great idea is for you to read your speech out loud as much as you can. Pick your time and place carefully, though. Public transport probably isn't a good idea – unless you're really insistent on having your own double seat. And speaking to yourself while walking down the street certainly gets you some funny looks.

But why not keep a copy of your speech next to the toilet? Every time you sit down, you can while away the minutes reading the speech out loud in privacy. Or take the speech with you when you walk the dog: At least you can be sure Pooch won't give away your best lines.

Speak easy: Get tuition

No one's expecting you to come across like Martin Luther King on the Lincoln Memorial steps. But if you really want to inject a bit of professionalism into your speech, why not consider a bit of coaching? The following websites offer advice and can help you choose a course:

www.collegeofpublic speaking.co.uk

http://speak-easily.com

www.speaking-infront.co.uk

www.the-asc.org.uk

www.professional speaking.biz

www.speak-first.com

Whether you're rehearsing your speech to a mirror, a camera or a friend, consider donning your wedding outfit while you're practising. You may be a bit self-conscious at first, but the rehearsal seems more authentic that way and ensures that you're more natural on the big day.

Fret Not

Every public speaker gets nervous before and during their speeches – even the world's greatest orators. The anxiety is what guarantees that they shine under pressure.

The difference between a good speaker and a bad one is how they channel that nervousness. Bad speakers feel weighed down by all the nervous energy, allowing this feeling to have a negative effect on their performance. But good speakers deflect their anxiety into positive nervous energy and use the feeling to boost their speech. Here are a few tips:

- ✔ **Do a final run through your speech 10 minutes before all the speeches are due to start.** Find a quiet area near the reception venue and read through your words quickly. You don't have to read them out loud – you just want to get them fresh in your mind.

- ✔ **Make sure that you know when and in which order the speeches are running** (I run through this in Chapter 7). As a general rule, you're third on after dinner. But check with the bride's father and the groom. You don't want any last-minute surprises – that won't help your nerves at all.

✔ **Build in time for a toilet break just before the speeches start.** If you're going to stand up in front of hundreds of guests, you want a clean face, tidy hair and an empty bladder. You need to consider the outside chance that the groom and the bride's father may bang on for hours. As the third speaker, you can hardly nip out in the middle of their speeches. And you don't want to deliver your speech cross-legged.

✔ **The final few seconds before you stand up to speak are crucial.** This point is when some public speakers get really stressed. If you're hot, mop your brow with a hand-kerchief. Take long deep breaths in and out to relax your body and mind. Clench and unclench your hands and feet. Don't worry – everyone's still watching the groom wrapping up his speech at this stage, so they won't notice what you're doing.

✔ **Look around at your audience.** They've been warmed up nicely by the two previous speakers. They've all got a few drinks inside them. They've had a few laughs, and they're looking forward to your speech. Be positive. Think how much they're going to cheer and laugh at your words. Imagine how proud the bride and groom are going to be and how much they're going to enjoy your words. Everyone's on your side and wants you to perform well. Even if you make mistakes in your delivery, they'll overlook them.

✔ **As you stand up to utter your opening line, think of something funny or happy.** Forget about how nervous you are and remember a hilarious time you had recently. Maybe it's a great joke you've just heard or something funny that happened to a friend of yours. This thought can make you smile and eradicate any nervousness for at least the first few seconds of your speech. Your face and body relax, and you can embark on your delivery with confidence. Your audience notice your smile and positive body language and relax with you.

✔ **Provided that your opening line gets some sort of reaction (which I cover in Chapter 8) – either a laugh or a cheer – use this moment as a springboard from which you can launch yourself into the main body of your speech.** A large audience actually works in your favour here. If your opening line gets only a little chuckle from each of the hundreds of guests, the individual chuckles can sound like a substantial laugh. This laughter can imbue you with confidence and see off any remaining nervousness.

✔ **Don't worry if your opening line doesn't work.** You may have totally misjudged your audience. Perhaps they didn't get your joke. Maybe the microphone didn't work – which happens to all the best speakers and stand-up comics at one time or another. Put this minor hiccup to the back of your mind and carry on with your speech. Don't let yourself be affected for the rest of your delivery.

✔ **Anxiety can make your mouth drier than brut champagne.** You can combat this feeling by keeping a glass of water handy to sip from every now and then during your speech.

✔ **Nervous speakers sometimes stammer or get a shaky voice.** You can cure this problem quickly: Slow down your speech and enunciate your words more precisely. The speech sounds better this way – especially to guests at the back of the room.

Delivering the Goods

You already look the part. Dolled up in your best man's suit, you cut a fine figure as you stand to deliver your speech. Importantly, now you need to back up your appearance with confident projection and body language. Even if your nerves are shot to pieces, you can use a few tricks to give the impression that you've got everything under control.

Making a stand

Stand up. Look bold. Look confident. A good stance is essential for a good speech. Barring those at the very front of the reception, for most of the guests, your body language consists primarily of the way you stand. Here are some pointers:

✔ Hold yourself upright, with your chin level (not too elevated or you look arrogant) and your shoulders back.

✔ Hold your speech or cue cards in one hand and the microphone in the other. If you're not using a mic, the other hand should be by your side.

✔ Place your feet shoulder-width apart. Instead of standing face-on to your audience, try placing one foot a few inches further forward than the other.

✔ Your natural inclination is to lock your knees and rest your weight on your heels. If you want to look dynamic and engage your audience more, bend your knees ever so slightly and shift your weight on to the balls of your feet. You may feel unnatural, but you'll be surprised how much more the guests hang on to your words.

Reception venues and marquees are often quite congested, especially when all the dinner tables are crammed in together. The room may not have a stage with a PA system, so you have to deliver your speech from behind your table. If you do have the chance, though, move out into an open space where all the guests can see you.

Hotel ballrooms and even some marquees have supporting pillars dotted around the middle of the floor. Usually at least one table of people, normally right at the back, doesn't have a direct view of the speaker. To get round this problem, vary your position from time to time during the speech. Don't pace up and down liked a caged tiger. But perhaps two or three times, at natural breaks in the speech, you can adjust your position by a few feet so that other guests get a better view. They'll appreciate a break in the routine.

The jury's out on whether hands in pockets during a speech is acceptable. In most cases, you're going to have only one hand free. If the wedding isn't very formal, then you may get away with an occasional relaxed dip into the pocket – perhaps while you tell a funny anecdote or during an impromptu part of the speech. You can even find this action comforting if you're a nervous speaker. But pocket usage must be occasional and never with both hands at once. Too much, and you look casual and disrespectful. On the whole, hands are better out than in.

Getting your audience on side

Right from the start, you want all the guests eating out of your hand. Unless you've got the stage presence of a rock star, you won't find achieving total control of the audience easy. But bear in mind that none of the guests wants your speech to flop. For three reasons, they want you to fare well:

- ✔ If you're uncomfortable or you mess things up, they feel uncomfortable, too.
- ✔ They want to laugh at your jokes.
- ✔ They want to feel good about the newly-weds and the wedding day.

Don't see your audience as one huge sea of faces. Your task can seem less daunting if you break up the group into individuals.

Just before you stand up to speak, single out three friendly faces among the guests – one on the right-hand side of the room, one in the middle and one on the left. If you can't spot three of your friends, search out people with happy smiley faces. Throughout the speech, these faces can be your focal points. Keep alternating your gaze from one of your chosen faces to the next. Try to make eye contact with them. Their smiles will fill you with confidence. This technique can also stop you from burying your head in your notes.

Your words need to be only the slightest bit funny for you to engage the guests. With a bellyful of wine, they chortle at jokes they'd normally only smile at.

Occasionally, you may find that some of your jokes fall flat. Don't worry – this situation happens to everyone, even the most experienced stand-up comics. Don't let a bad joke throw you. Simply move on to the next part of your speech.

If you find that you're starting to lose the attention of some of the guests, one sure way of reeling them back in is to do the following: In a loud voice, address a question to everyone that you're sure will result in a positive response. Shout out something like 'Isn't the bride the most beautiful you've ever seen?' or 'Isn't this the best wedding you've ever been to?' Even the bored guests at the back are going to stop chatting to join in the resulting cheer.

Keeping it slow

Anxiety makes a lot of speakers canter through their speech as fast as they possibly can. Subconsciously, they're thinking 'The sooner I get through my address, the sooner I can get off the stage and out of the limelight.'

But that doesn't help out the audience at all. If you want them to appreciate every word – and come on, you took hours to write this speech – then you have to slow down your delivery. Pause between sentences. Stop and look up at your audience. Read the key phrases or quotations even more slowly and deliberately. The change in pace lends weight to your words and stop your speech sounding like one long monologue.

Throwing your voice

No one wants a shouty Reverend Ian Paisley-style address. But everyone present must be able to hear what you've got to say. A microphone can take care of the volume – you have to raise your voice considerably if one isn't provided. To stop your sentences from tailing off and to make sure that all the guests catch your every word, you need to enunciate everything clearly.

Accentuate the movements of your mouth as you speak. In normal conversation, we tend to mumble a bit or let the final few words of a phrase fall away. This method of speaking is fine when the person you're talking to is just a couple of feet away. But imagine what it's like for the slightly deaf old guests at the back of the marquee. They haven't got a chance.

 When you come to speaking in public, work on the lowest common denominator. If the people at the back of the reception can hear clearly what you're saying, you can guarantee that everyone else can, too. Near the start of your speech, address a group of people sitting right at the back to check whether they can hear properly. If you're also master of ceremonies (MC) (refer to Chapter 7 for more on this role), you need to check the situation before all the speeches start. The guests soon pipe up if the acoustics are no good. After all, no one wants to sit through half an hour of speeches barely catching a word.

Taking the mic

If you're going to work with a PA system, familiarise yourself with the microphone well before the speeches start. You want to avoid looking like an idiot when your turn comes to speak. Remember that wedding PAs are notoriously temperamental. Be prepared to do without if the system's not functioning properly.

Often, a technically minded friend of the groom is in charge of the PA. At the beginning of the reception, ask him to show you how to turn on the mic and adjust the stand. You're probably not going to swing the mic round your head like Freddie Mercury, but a bit of stage planning won't go amiss.

Don't get so cocky that you turn down the option of using the microphone altogether. Even small reception rooms have bad acoustics at the back of the room. A microphone projects your voice all around the room and stops your sentences from tailing off, which can make the difference between a joke everyone laughs at and one nobody hears.

Ideally, your mouth needs to be about 20 centimetres away from the head of the microphone when you speak. This distance avoids distortion but means that all your words are picked up. Remember that the mic is an amplifier, not something to hide behind. Move the stand slightly to the side of your body so that you look more like a public speaker and less like Oasis in concert.

If you have a microphone but no stand, don't be tempted to wave the thing about as you move your hands. To pick up your voice, the mic needs to be near your mouth at all times.

Occasionally during your speech, try removing the mic from the stand. Pause, walk a few paces to another position, and carry on talking with the mic held to your mouth. This technique is a good way to emphasise key sentences in your speech and, for the guests, it breaks up the monotony of seeing you in just one place. Later, at a natural pause in the speech, you can return the mic to its stand.

Making your moves

Different orators have different physical styles in front of a crowd. Politicians often push their hands forward while they speak – partly as a defence barrier and partly to get their message across. Princess Diana was demure and almost motionless. Adolf Hitler couldn't open his mouth without saluting the sky. But the point is that despite their vastly differing stage manners, all three orators mentioned come across as very effective speakers.

When you come to do *your* speech, you're better off playing safe. By all means use your hands to convey certain points. And changing your standing position two or three times during your delivery is not a bad thing (check out 'Making a stand' earlier in this chapter). But don't gesticulate or move about unnecessarily – this movement puts off the guests and distracts them from what you're saying.

Nerves can cause funny little tics in public speakers. Some speakers keep pushing back their hair, others scratch their chin, some fiddle with their notes and others play with the rings on their fingers. Prince Charles is a notable case: He's continually fiddling with his cuff and dipping his hand into his jacket pocket when he talks.

You don't want the guests concentrating more on what you're doing with your hands than on the words you're speaking. By practising your speech into a camcorder (refer to 'You've been framed' earlier in this chapter), you can iron out these tics before the big day.

Making notes

The best speeches are memorised speeches. If you learn your lines, you can look at the guests the whole time. Eye contact is a great way to get them on your side. You won't need to look down at any notes, and your words have better rhythm and seem far more natural.

But most of us mortals need to print the speech on paper. As a compromise, why not partially memorise the speech and use bullet points written on cue cards as an aide-memoire? (I remind you about this in Chapter 8.)

Sheets of A4 flap about and shake in your hands if you're really nervous. Small cue cards are far less conspicuous.

Toning up your speaking skills

The tone in which you deliver your speech depends on your surroundings. A Buckingham Palace reception is going to require a vastly more formal style than the public lounge at your local pub. As best man, you have a better idea than most about the guests who are watching you. In the run-up to the wedding, check with the groom and the bride's father so you can gauge the formality of the whole reception and adapt your tone accordingly.

Don't put on airs. People see through any pretence immediately. Be natural, not stilted. You can speak in a conversational tone without sounding disrespectful. Just cut down a touch on the slang.

If you've got a strong regional accent, don't try to disguise it. At least half of the guests are likely to know, or know of, you. What are you trying to hide? If the bride and groom were ashamed of your speaking voice, they wouldn't have picked you as best man.

The aspects of your voice that you need to spruce up a bit are the pace, pitch, stress and volume. Rattling off your piece in the same flat monotone means that by the end of your speech, you can expect to be competing with the snores of half the guests.

Here are some tips on keeping your audience attentive:

- ✔ **Vary the volume:** For effect, read some parts with a bellow and some with just a loud whisper. Choose the right bits, though.

- ✔ **Impersonations:** If you quote someone, try to copy their accent and style of speaking.

- ✔ **Vary the pace:** Most of your speech can be slow and methodical (see 'Keeping it slow' earlier in this chapter), but you can accentuate certain parts with rapid-fire delivery.

- ✔ **Vary the pitch:** Speak very high in some parts and very low in others. This method can add to the comic effect of an anecdote.

Preparing props

Treat props with the utmost caution. Get them right, and
you can create great comic effect. Get them wrong, and you
fall flat on your face. The trick is to keep them simple and
instantly recognisable.

You may have an overwhelming desire to illustrate an anecdote with a photograph of the groom. But if only the few
people at the front of the room can see the picture, this prop
won't work. If you want to use projected images or video,
make sure that everyone can see the screen. You need to have
a clear idea in advance of the layout of the venue and the positions of the guests' tables.

Always beware of technology as machines have a habit of
going awry at the crucial moment. If you're planning to use
a music or video player or a projector, familiarise yourself
thoroughly with the hardware well before the speeches start.
Even better, you can get a technical friend to take charge of
the machinery for you. You've got quite enough on your plate
without having to worry about wires and buttons.

With a bit of research, you should be able to dig up some
highly embarrassing photos or film footage of the groom. The
best man's speech is the perfect opportunity to display this
material to everyone who knows him.

If you've been friends with the groom for a long time, you may
well have loads of visual material yourself. Photos and videos
from school and college are often hilarious. Ask members of
his family if they've got stuff you can borrow. You can always
transfer the material to the same format for easy broadcasting
during your speech.

With a computer and the right software, you can create your
own video or slide shows. Link up a laptop to a large TV
screen, and you're going to be able to lampoon the groom
publicly. Otherwise, high-street photography shops can digi-
tise old print photos for you. Whatever format you end up
using, laughs are guaranteed.

Collect funny photos of the groom at every stage of his life,
from birth all the way up to the engagement party. His family
and oldest friends will enjoy helping you with this. Run them

in chronological order and accompany each one with a verbal caption. If he never forgives you, then you've done a good job. Tempted as you may be, you're better off leaving out photos from the stag do.

Childhood toys, security blankets, old school reports, embarrassing items from his wardrobe – the possibilities are endless. You need a bit of collusion from his family to help you out, but these props are well worth the effort.

Involving the audience

Audience participation is a great way to get things going. Guests are going to appreciate being able to contribute to the speeches.

The awards ceremony

To make the guests feel involved in the speech, why not invent some awards and hand out trophies for certain categories? Here are some ideas:

- ✒ The guest who first introduced the bride and groom to each other
- ✒ The guest who travelled the furthest to be there
- ✒ The oldest friends of the bride and groom
- ✒ The guest in the smartest suit
- ✒ The guest wearing the best hat
- ✒ The guest who sent the best invitation RSVP

If you really want to do things properly, warn the recipients beforehand so that they can prepare short acceptance speeches.

Don't get your heckles up

Not all audience participation is welcome. Hecklers are every public speaker's nightmare. You can be in full stride, regaling your audience with the most scintillating speech imaginable. Suddenly, some smart Alec pipes up with what they think is a witty comment, and you lose your momentum and all your confidence. Few things are more distracting.

The multiple key trick

A few days before the wedding, buy ten blank keys from a key cutter. Just before the speeches start, hand them out to ten pretty female guests and tell them to put them in their pockets and to keep shtum. During your speech, announce to everyone that the bride has agreed to forget about all the groom's past relationships. Water under the bridge, so to speak. She knows he was quite a ladies' man, but as a special amnesty, she now wants any former girlfriends among the guests to hand back any keys to her husband's place that they may still have. At this juncture, the ten lovely ladies should walk up to the top table, and each hand their key over to the bride. For extra effect, you may want to include a couple of grannies among the young beauties.

What you have to remember is that at a wedding, everyone's on your side. Hecklers aren't trying to put you off. They just want to join in and prove to everyone else that they're funny, too. And they're probably jealous of all the attention you're getting.

Nothing's wrong with indulging them a little bit. Thank any hecklers for their contribution, almost as if you had expected them to interrupt all along. Try not to seem rattled by them. They are likely to be a friend of yours, so why not acknowledge them by name? That way they're sure to have the 15 seconds of fame they so obviously desire.

Don't get into a protracted conversation with a heckler; otherwise, your speech can lose its momentum. If they continue to heckle, say something like, 'Look, I'd love to stand here and talk all day with you, but I've got a rather important speech to finish. Can we continue this at the bar afterwards?'

Remember that you're not a stand-up comedian. Don't try to outwit a heckler or put them down with witty one-liners. This move may end up backfiring. Just let them have their say, acknowledge them and move on.

Part IV
The Part of Tens

In this part . . .

✔ Get some instant ideas on where to go on the stag do – both locally and globally.

✔ Discover fun, thrilling activities that get everyone involved and united.

✔ Avoid the things that *can* go wrong.

Chapter 10

Ten Great Ideas for the Stag Do

In This Chapter

▶ Having fun in the United Kingdom and abroad

▶ Sporting and active days out

▶ Drinking and gambling

*Y*ou may only have the budget for a curry and a pub crawl. Or perhaps you and the groom are feeling flash, and you're planning to whisk everyone off to Eastern Europe for the weekend. Whatever you choose to do, be sure to let your hair down, enjoy yourselves and send the groom off in style.

If you're stuck for inspiration, here are ten of the best stag do ideas. Some suggestions are cheap, some are super-expensive. But they're all guaranteed fun.

Tee Time

Golf is the great equaliser. Because of the handicap system, you can pitch Tiger Woods against a weekend hacker and still even things out.

Avoid the more upmarket courses. With a large group of rowdy stags, you're only going to end up aggravating the other members. You may even get thrown off the course if you misbehave too much.

You can play many different variations of golf, depending on the time available and the skill level of the players. (Check out

Chapter 2.) And if shots start to go really awry, you've always got the 19th hole to look forward to.

Fuelling Your Imagination

For all you petrolheads out there, an afternoon thrashing round the racetrack in a beast of a fast car takes a lot of beating. Unfortunately, participating in this outing means that each stag spends most of his time on his own, but it's great for the adrenalin rush.

A variety of vehicles are on offer: single seaters, sports cars, touring cars or whatever tickles your fancy. At some racetracks, you can even indulge in a spot of off-road rally driving as well.

The following tracks are open to the public:

- **Brands Hatch** (www.brandshatch.co.uk; 01474-872331).

- **Castle Combe Circuit** (www.castlecombecircuit.co.uk; 01249-782929)

- **Rockingham Circuit** (www.rockingham.co.uk; 01536 500500)

- **Silverstone** (www.silverstone.co.uk; 0844 3750740)

- **Thruxton Motor Sport Centre** (www.thruxtonracing.co.uk; 01264-882222)

Monopoly Board Pub Crawl

One for the London-based stags – though versions of Monopoly do exist for other cities – this do requires very little organisation. It's perfect for the kind of best man for whom the proverbial gathering in a brewery poses logistical challenges. All you need is a tube pass, an A-to-Z, a strong drinking arm and the constitution of an ox.

The idea works like this: Your mission is to drink a pint (or half a pint, if you want to remember the event afterwards) in a pub on every street featured on the Monopoly board. To take the original London version as the basis, you start in Old Kent Road and finish 22 streets later in Mayfair. If you're really hard core, you can have a drink at the stations featured, too. But don't cheat by knocking off several neighbouring streets all at once: To do this pub crawl properly, you've got to visit the pubs in order.

Bearing in mind the original Monopoly's pre-War origins, you have several anomalies to contend with. No Marlborough Street exists in central London – only a Great Marlborough Street. Mayfair isn't a street, but an area. The Angel Islington is a junction of several roads, not one, and many of the streets (Northumberland Avenue, Pall Mall, Vine Street and Trafalgar Square) don't have pubs on them at all. The newer version of the Monopoly board doesn't suffer from these problems.

Before the United Kingdom's pub opening hours changed in the mid-2000s, the time constraints used to be the major problem. If you started the crawl at 11 a.m. and finished at 11 p.m., that meant 22 pubs in 12 hours (32 minutes per pub, including traveling time). But now that you're allowed to drink into the wee hours, your mission is a lot easier to accomplish.

Argy Bargey: Hiring a Barge

For a slightly more relaxed stag weekend, why not hire a narrow boat for a weekend and cruise the canals of Britain? The Norfolk Broads, Bath, Merseyside, North Wales, Stoke on Trent, Glasgow to Edinburgh, north London . . . the routes are endless. 'Waterway to have a good time' . . . as Alan Partridge once said.

War! What Is It Good for?

If guns, war and playing soldiers is what you're after, then why not go the whole hog and sign everyone up for a military training day? Eastern Europe is ripe for the picking.

Ever since the demise of communism across the former Eastern Bloc, hundreds of ex-servicemen have been sitting around twiddling their thumbs (and the safety catches on their Kalashnikovs). The threat from the evil West has gone, and many of these countries are now part of the European Union, anyway. Their trigger-happy former soldiers love nothing better than showing a bunch of lily-livered stags what being in the army is really like. Just make sure that you've checked the small print in your travel insurance policy before you go.

Some stag organisers offer military training. Sunshine World (www.sunshineworld.co.uk; 020 7581 4736), for example, offers tank driving, shooting Kalashnikovs, abseiling and rappelling in Poland.

Try to bring the stag back home alive.

The Sky's the Limit: Sky Diving

To avoid spending hours training for your jump (no stag's going to have the patience for that), you're best off opting for a tandem jump with an instructor. That way you can be in the air after a few minutes rather than a few hours.

This activity tends to be pricey, and some of the stags may need a bit of persuasion to go through with the jump, but you can guarantee no one's going to forget the experience quickly.

Contact the British Parachute Association (www.bpa.org.uk; 0116-278-5271) for more information.

The Big Blue

The problem with a lot of stag activities is that everyone gets split up throughout the day. Not so with deep sea fishing. Crammed together on a see-sawing skiff all day, you'll certainly get to know one another a lot better. And you can laugh at the groom as he desperately tries to land his catch: seaweed, a boot, an old shopping trolley . . . anything

Be warned, however – hangovers and rough seas don't mix.

Viva Las Vegas

The United Kingdom's rapidly relaxing gambling laws mean that casinos are springing up all over the country. Although you may have to sign everyone in as members in advance, you can't really fail to have a good time: Suits, cocktails and the fear of losing tons of cash injects excitement into even the most pedestrian stag do. Just don't let the groom run off with the kitty.

The Beautiful Game

One of the main purposes of the stag do is to get all the groom's mates bonding together. Team sport is the perfect catalyst for this. All around the country, almost every weekend, five-, six- and seven-a-side football tournaments take place, open to any team of any ability – champs or chumps.

If you have a large stag party, you can split the group into several teams. Make sure that the groom and you, the best man, are captains, though.

Contact the Football Association (www.thefa.com) for more information.

Getting Festive

All over Europe, festivals are held throughout the year that celebrate anything from tomato farming to folk music. But one thing they all have in common is that proceedings tend to be lubricated by booze.

Check out the following annual events:

- ✔ Sanfermin, Pamplona, Spain, July: Run with the bulls! See www.sanfermin.com.
- ✔ Oktoberfest, Munich, Germany, September and October: Oompah, oompah, steins of beer and so on. See www.Oktoberfest.de/en.

- La Tomatina, Bunol, Spain, August: A mass food fight with tomatoes.

- Glastonbury Festival, Worthy Farm, Pilton, Somerset, UK, June: See www.glastonburyfestivals.co.uk.

- Notting Hill Carnival, London, August: All the best of the Caribbean.

- The Exit Festival, Novi Sad, Serbia, July: Dance the night away. See www.exitfest.org.

- Edinburgh International Festival, Edinburgh, UK, July and August: Comedy, theatre and general shenanigans. See www.edinburghfestivals.co.uk.

- Guca Festival, Guca, Serbia, August: Brass band heaven. See www.guca.rs.

- Speyside Whisky Festival, Moray and Speyside, UK, May: Fancy a wee dram? See www.spiritofspeyside.com.

- Feria du Riz, Arles, France, September: Bullfights, sangria, and paella. See www.feriaarles.com.

Chapter 11

Ten Best Stag Do Destinations

In This Chapter

▶ Discovering great venues in the United Kingdom

▶ Exploring perfect stag cities in the rest of Europe

*T*hanks to cheap short-haul air travel, you now have dozens of destinations – some glamorous, some downright tacky – available to stag parties. In many of them, local businesses have geared themselves up specially to cater for this market, and in the early summer months (the high stag season), the local economy very much depends on these trips.

Here are ten great stag destinations (five of them in the British Isles and five in continental Europe) where you're guaranteed to have a great time.

London, United Kingdom

Samuel Johnson famously reminded us that once you get bored of Britain's capital, you might as well just go out and shoot yourself. The same very much goes for stags. More pubs, clubs, restaurants and casinos exist than anywhere else in the country – and very nearly anywhere else in Europe. In fact, if apart from Paris and Rome, Londoners could argue that theirs is the most important city across the continent – historically and culturally, anyway. Not that stags are ever too concerned about history and culture.

Newquay, United Kingdom

The West Country's surf capital is also a party capital. During the summer, thousands of revellers, including numerous rowdy stags and hens, descend upon the poor town, intent on finding the answer to life at the bottom of several glasses. Pubs, nightclubs and cheap group accommodations abound, some of which are too tacky for words. The main streets of the town are not for the faint-hearted – weekend evenings can resemble something of a war zone – but if you want to hit the beaches by day and the tiles by night, then this city's perfect.

Slightly out of town, things calm down a little. Here you find the classier hotels and restaurants, and you won't have to block out loud, repetitive beats in order to get to sleep. And don't forget: Cornwall has some of the most beautiful beaches in the whole of the British Isles.

Brighton, United Kingdom

Brighton lights up the south coast like a beacon, and, during the summer months especially, that beacon rarely dims. You can find enough bars and nightclubs to satisfy even the wildest party animal. Your only problem may be keeping tabs on all the stags as they lose themselves down the Lanes – that's local terminology for the narrow backstreets of the town centre.

The stony beach is a hive of activity during daylight hours, while Brighton Pier has fruit machines and fairground rides. The city itself has all the sophistication and style of London, but without the prices, hectic lifestyle and brusqueness of the inhabitants.

Nottingham, United Kingdom

On a Saturday night, the centre of Nottingham pulsates with the thunder of dance music and the splash of rapidly filling pint glasses. As the United Kingdom's city with the highest concentration of pubs and clubs, this Midlands venue isn't always a pretty sight, but if your ideal stag party involves boozing and dancing, then you're in heaven.

You won't find a shortage of female company, either: Apparently, women outnumber men by four to one. As for dressing up the stag, why not put him in a pair of tights and a silly hat – worked for Robin Hood. And all his men were certainly merry.

Barcelona, Spain

Local police are cracking down on public rowdiness, especially along the bustling human theatre that is Las Ramblas. But nothing dampens the Spaniards' desire to party every night of the week. You've always tomorrow's siesta to catch up on your sleep.

The city is expensive compared to the rest of Spain, but with a bit of Internet research, you can check into one of the many hotels that cater to large groups. Some even feature dormitories for the seriously cash-strapped tourist.

You can find plenty to do during daylight hours, too. Camp Nou, home of Barcelona FC, is a short metro ride from the city centre, and every Sunday during the summer, bullfighting is held at the Plaza de Toros Monumental. You can't get more macho than that.

Tallinn, Estonia

Several airlines link directly from United Kingdom airports to the Estonian capital, which means that you don't have to waste too much of the stag weekend travelling. Once you get there, you soon realize why this city is considered one of Eastern Europe's most vibrant stag destinations. Many travel companies are now specializing in stag parties operating in the city.

As well as the quaint medieval architecture and cobbled streets, you also find multifarious stag activities on offer, including snow karting on a frozen lake in winter, beach action in summer and military training days all year round. For the seriously masochistic, you'll even find a bar that plays nothing but Depeche Mode songs all day, every day. But be warned: Winters in Tallinn are vicious. The wind whips off the Baltic Sea, and no amount of vodka can protect you from the cold.

Berlin, Germany

Isolated from the rest of their compatriots during the Cold War, Berliners have always been a bit different. Their idea of having a good time is no exception. They certainly know how to put away a beer and love partying into the wee hours. Their warehouse-sized nightclubs, in particular, are legendary. Getting your head round German techno just takes a bit of time.

Amsterdam, Holland

Everyone always chuckles and winks when you say, 'I spent the weekend in Amsterdam'. Given the locals' liberal attitude towards both nudity and narcotics, that's hardly surprising. While the city's infamous cafés and red light district won't be every stag's cup of tea, everything you may want is there. Cheap accommodation is available, and hoteliers are quite used to catering to large groups of young men. Just remember that, as best man, you're responsible for getting the stag home in one piece . . . and with his morals intact.

Prague, Czech Republic

The Czech capital is not as stag-friendly as it once was – mainly because the locals have tired of seeing young men make fools of themselves on their streets. Prices have also increased massively in response to the tourist influx from Western Europe. But if you want to have a great party against the backdrop of one of the most beautiful cities on the continent, then this city is your venue. Watch out for the legendary absinthe, though – doesn't always do what it says on the bottle.

Dublin, Irish Republic

Memories of Dublin tend to get somewhat clouded after excess Guinness. But the Irish capital has so much more to offer than just the black stuff. As well as some of the friendliest locals in Western Europe and a thriving live music scene, you can spend some great evenings hanging out in Temple Bar, home of the city's most exciting bars and clubs.

Add to this the fact that budget airlines can fly you over for less than the price of a taxi ride – and that you're in a foreign country without the language barrier – and you soon see why Dublin is such a popular stag destination.

Chapter 12

Ten Wedding Nightmare Scenarios

* *

In This Chapter

▶ Dealing with nightmare problems

▶ Avoiding tricky situations

* *

*1*n an ideal world, none of the things mentioned in this chapter would happen. The entire wedding process would go swimmingly, the happy couple would glide into wedded bliss and you would turn out to be the perfect best man.

But we don't live in an ideal world. Cock-ups are certain to happen at one stage or another. If you avoid the ones listed here, then you've done well.

Stag Do Injuries

Shaved eyebrows and the odd black eye are just about passable. As long as you hold the stag party long enough before the big day, they have the time to, at least partially, grow back or heal.

But broken limbs are another matter. While a fractured fibia won't stop the groom from being able to say 'I do', the bride won't be at all happy if his ring finger's wrapped up in a sling. And since you're in charge of the stag do, you're going to be blamed. Perhaps that military training day in Kabul wasn't such a great idea after all.

Lose the Ring

If Frodo managed to get all the way to Mordor without losing his ring, then you should be able to get your groom's wedding ring as far as the altar. The trouble is that wedding days are often more perilous than epic journeys across Middle-earth. And you haven't even got Gollum and the Orcs to deal with!

Remember that classic scene in the 1994 film *Four Weddings and a Funeral* when Hugh Grant loses the ring at the crucial moment? This scene is just one of hundreds of similar celluloid tales all designed to alert best men of the pitfalls of mislaying the most important object of the entire day. Be warned.

No-Show Bride, No-Show Groom

With a bit of inventiveness, you can just about cope with most wedding absentees. If the band doesn't turn up, use a stereo. If the photographer's late, then pose for photos in the evening. If the vicar's ill, then get a replacement from a nearby church. If you lose the ring, use a Hula Hoop.

But without either the bride or the groom, no wedding can possibly take place. The event just ain't happening. Luckily for you, long gone are the days when the best man or the chief bridesmaid had to step in as replacements. Nowadays, a no-show bride or groom means game over.

If the groom is the one who has done a runner, you're responsible for both trying to find him and for breaking the news to the bride and her family.

Ceremony Interruption

At 99.9 per cent of weddings, you always get an awkward silence when the vicar asks all those present if they know of any reason why the couple shouldn't be allowed to marry. 'Speak now or forever hold your peace!' he proclaims to the congregation. At which point everyone holds their breath, not quite sure whether someone might dare pipe up.

Aside from the occasional bored toddler, no one ever does – except in films. But if someone did burst into the church, like Dustin Hoffman in *The Graduate,* imagine the chaos that would ensue.

Wedding Fight

Every wedding has a fight, even if two page boys just start squabbling over who's getting the biggest piece of cake. However, things get slightly scarier when the protagonists are larger . . . and drunker. The sight of two men wrestling on the dance floor in hired penguin suits is not a pretty one – especially, when *Dancing Queen* is blaring out of the stereo. And don't go running for the shelter of the bar. As best man, you're expected to help break things up.

Speech Embarrassments

Over the years, some downright cringe-worthy speeches have been delivered at wedding receptions. Speakers have used their minutes in the spotlight to reveal embarrassing details that, in the cold light of dawn, they realise simply should have remained unsaid.

Normally the revelations concern other members of the wedding party. The worst one of all was the groom who wrapped up his speech by drawing two honeymoon aeroplane tickets from his breast pocket, handing them to his bride and best man sitting beside him, and then publicly announced that he'd known all along they were having an affair behind his back.

Needless to say, don't even go there.

Drunken Guests

An afternoon of flowing champagne and an evening of free bar service spells disaster for some guests. You can always spot them at receptions – they're the ones weaving their way in between the tables and dancing vigorously to Abba with a bottle in each hand. Just as long as they stay merry and don't get abusive (or start singing), you shouldn't have too much trouble. But your job as best man is to keep an eye out for anyone who gets too plastered.

Dodgy Weather

The summer months in the United Kingdom are notoriously unreliable when the weather is concerned. This reason is why marquee weddings are so widespread. But even with a huge white tent to shelter under, the wedding party still has to negotiate between the church and the reception. And in a rainstorm, this task is not easy.

When the weather's wet, the back garden (or wherever the marquee's situated) can soon turn into a quagmire. Fortunately, rainy weddings are considered good luck. Try telling that to the bride, though, whose wedding dress train has been dragged across a muddy lawn.

Family Feuding

At most weddings, the families of the bride and groom are generally very civil. Even if potential clashes are possible, the relatives normally manage to prevent them from bubbling over. But occasionally, the emotion and stress of the whole day, not to mention the booze, all conspire to cause interfamilial strife.

 If both the bride's and the groom's mother have turned out in identical dresses, take this fact as a sure sign that things may go awry.

Avoiding Temptation

Another wedding cliché is that while the bride and groom are swooning over one another in wedded bliss, the romance of the whole occasion starts to infect other members of the wedding party. There you are, standing next to the groom, all smart in your suit, and suddenly you start noticing amorous glances coming from the bridesmaids. Don't even go there.

Chapter 13

Ten Great Budget Stag Tips

In This Chapter

▶ Having fun without breaking the bank

▶ Exploring budget versions of traditional stag parties

The world may be full of economic doom, but that doesn't mean you can't celebrate the end of your groom's bachelorhood in style. Perhaps you simply need to reign in the spending a bit.

The major expenses on any stag party are accommodation, travel and booze. You can hardly economise on the latter – much better to avoid splashing out on the other two. So if you really want to keep prices low, throw a party near your home town and avoid overnight stays in a hotel. The following ten tips will make sure even the most skint stags have a great time.

Life's a Beach

On a tight budget, there's no way you're going to be partying on the Med. But there's no reason why you shouldn't throw the mother of all beach parties. Just choose a seaside resort near the stag's home town.

You'll need lots of booze, meat, a portable BBQ and a music player. Opt for a remote beach, and you may get away with building a huge bonfire to stay warm. Why not bring tents and extend it into an overnight camping trip? All said, you could probably budget for £25 a head plus travel costs.

Master Chef

If you can't afford to travel, then why not bring the party to you? Suggest that the groom hosts an amazing dinner party at his own house and invite an amateur chef to cater for everyone.

We all know someone who fancies himself as a culinary genius. Well, here's your chance to bring out his inner Master Chef. What's required is a lot of flattery and a bit of bribery: Approach a friend (not one invited to the stag party) who thinks he's a god in the kitchen and offer him cash to cook a Michelin-star dinner for all the stags. (£200 should cover ingredients and labour which, split between all the stags, will work out a lot cheaper than any restaurant.)

Then ask every stag to bring along a rather special bottle of wine . . . or two. (The chef will give you guidance on what region and grape to opt for.) The resulting dinner party will be better than anything you might expect in a commercial restaurant. Plus, there's the added benefit that you can misbehave without incurring the wrath of fellow diners.

Raise You!

Head for a casino, and you're likely to blow most of the evening's budget within minutes. So what about hosting a poker night at the stag's house? That way you can ensure no one loses huge amounts of money.

Of course, you want some element of gambling. Otherwise, poker is nothing more than pushing cards around a table. But if you use matches instead of real cash, there's no chance anyone will head home in tears. Suggest that every stag buys £20 worth of matches at the start of the evening and perhaps offer a grand prize for the overall winner.

The other advantage of hosting the game at the stag's house is that you can enjoy cheap cognac and cigars. Instead of Hennessy XO and Cohibas, opt for house brandy and Honduran cigars. That should work out at just £15 a head before you all turn green.

A Rambling We Will Go

This one all hinges on the infamous British weather. Choose the right weekend, and a 15-mile yomp across the moors can be bliss. Choose the wrong weekend, and you'll be wet and miserable.

The trick is to find a hiking route with lots of pub stops along the way. That way, should the clouds start rolling in, you've got a dry plan B.

While active stags will love the idea of hiking for miles, inactive ones might see it as torture. So keep daily distances fairly short and choose a path that is well way-marked. There are some classic long-distance routes in this country: South Downs Way, Pennine Way, Pembrokeshire Coast Path, Ridgeway, South West Coast Path and Hadrian's Wall Path are all good. And you don't need to hike the whole length – a short section will suffice.

If you want to make a weekend of it, youth hostels or bed and breakfast accommodation ranges between £20 and £30 per person per night. Just be sure you don't let slip that it's a stag party. Landladies won't be happy.

X Marks the Spot

Nothing like a treasure hunt to bring out the pirate in you. Whether you're all hiking across the countryside or chasing round a city centre, a treasure hunt is a great way to test the brains and brawn of all the stags.

You've got several options here. Either you join a well-established treasure-hunt organisation, such as Geocaching (www.geocaching.com), or you pay a treasure-hunt company to devise a personalised hunt specially for your stag party.

Geocaching is the cheapest way to do it. This is an outdoor game where you use GPS coordinates to locate hidden containers. There are containers hidden all over the world, in towns and across the countryside. To play, you simply visit the website, download the app (US$9.99 for the iPhone one when we went to press) and get searching – near wherever you happen to be holding the stag party.

If you fancy something more personalised, then you could hire the services of a treasure-hunt organiser. For a fee (it's normally negotiable), the organiser will tailor-make a treasure hunt in your local area, perhaps with a theme that appeals to the groom.

Try the following organisers:

- ✔ The Treasure Hunt Company (www.treasurehunts.co.uk; 0845 006 0606)

- ✔ Treasure Hunts UK (www.treasurehuntsuk.com; 01790 756940)

- ✔ Wildgoose Treasure Hunts (www.huntthegoose.co.uk; 0845 838 2402)

- ✔ Treasure Trails (www.treasuretrails.co.uk)

- ✔ Huntfun (www.huntfun.co.uk)

- ✔ UK: The Game (www.ukthegame.com; 0845 0942931)

Out of Your League

Premier League football will certainly get the pulses racing, but once you've forked out for tickets to get all the stags into a Chelsea versus Manchester United match, you won't have much change left from a grand. What about aiming your sights slightly lower and switching allegiance to a nonleague team? Maybe the stag's local club?

Granted, you'll be watching 22 plumbers kick a pig's bladder round a bumpy field, but it will work out very cheap indeed. With security much slacker than you'd find at a Premier League ground, you can probably smuggle in your own beers, too.

Visit the Ryman League website (http://rymanleague.goalrun.com) to find a nonleague club near you. At this level, you'll rarely pay more than £10 each for a ticket. Nor should you, given the skill on display.

Pub Olympics

Pub sports all have one thing in common: You can still compete with multiple pints inside you. The key is to choose a pub that features lots of sports facilities and one where you can ask the landlord to reserve them for your stag party.

Pool, darts and table football are the obvious ones – a quick Internet search will pinpoint which local pubs have them. But to stage a genuine pub Olympics, you're going to need more sports than that. What about dominoes, Jenga, draughts or backgammon? In some regions, pubs have a skittles alley out the back. You'll also need a couple of drinking games just to keep everyone well-oiled (see Chapter 14).

Make sure any sports you include are quick and easy to play; otherwise, you risk losing the attention of the stags. For this reason, knock-out competitions are always better than round-robin ones. If it's a large stag party, you may want to split the group into two-man teams to save time. And appoint one person (possibly you, as best man) as referee. Offer prizes for the overall gold, silver and bronze winners.

Posh Picnic

Another weather-dependent one, this. But on a nice summer's day, and with the right location, you can't beat a boozy picnic.

Just make sure it's a very posh one. Look online for some great deals on cases of Champagne – you can get the real stuff for as low as £12 a bottle if you shop around. And what about some caviar, smoked salmon and foie gras? Ask each stag to chip in £30, and you'll have a lunch fund big enough to really impress.

Better than Hitch-Hiking

Public transport across the UK is unreliable and expensive. Depending on where you all live, a trip to the Highlands of Scotland, for example, could easily set you back more than £200 per person in train fares.

Much better to hire a minibus and all drive together to your stag destination. This guarantees that the party starts the minute you hit the road. And to avoid designated drivers, you might consider hiring a chauffeur as well.

Cheap minibus hire starts at around £80 a day – considerably more if you need a driver, too.

Your Name Is on the List

A Michael McIntyre show followed by a U2 concert – wouldn't that make for a great stag party? The problem is it would cost close to £250 per head just for the tickets.

That doesn't mean Cinderella won't go to the ball, however. In cities all over the UK, with a bit of research, you can find free gigs and comedy shows in various pubs and clubs. Granted, the quality won't quite be up there with McIntyre and U2, but you'll still be entertained.

The following websites advertise free gigs, live shows and TV shows:

- ✔ www.free-events.co.uk
- ✔ www.timeout.com
- ✔ www.allgigs.co.uk
- ✔ www.youngandpoor.co.uk
- ✔ www.bbc.co.uk/comedy
- ✔ www.sroaudiences.com
- ✔ www.applausestore.com
- ✔ www.hattrick.co.uk/ticketing
- ✔ www.beonlive.com
- ✔ www.lostintv.com
- ✔ www.spoonfed.co.uk
- ✔ www.comedy.co.uk

Chapter 14

Ten Great Drinking Games

In This Chapter

▶ Having fun while drinking

▶ Dice games, card games, games of dexterity and TV games

Drinking games aren't big, and they aren't clever. But they certainly are a lot of fun, especially on stag parties. If, at some point during the evening, you feel the celebrations are flagging, you may want to inject a bit of excitement by suggesting a drinking game. There's a good mix of ideas here, ranging from dice games and tests of manual or verbal dexterity to straightforward noisy fun.

Most require the players to perform a certain task. Fail in that task, and you are normally expected to drink a forfeit. Of course, you don't want the evening to end too soon, so make sure the drinking forfeit is fairly small – perhaps a two-finger's-width slug of booze. It's perfectly reasonable to expect the groom to drink double forfeits. It is, after all, his party.

If nondrinkers are in attendance (unlikely on a stag do), you can always impose non-alcoholic forfeits instead. Perhaps get the loser to perform 30 press-ups in front of everyone. Or force him to accept a dead-arm punch from all the other stags. It's up to you, as best man, to decide on the alternative forfeits.

Be warned, though. Drinking to excess can be dangerous. As best man, you have a responsibility to ensure the groom doesn't finish the evening unconscious and handcuffed.

The Cocktail from Hell

You'll need a stomach of steel for this one. On a sheet of paper, write down the names of six spirits and six mixers, numbering them one to six. Now ask the stag to roll two dice to decide which spirit will feature in the special cocktail and which mixer will accompany it.

Once you've got the two ingredients, ask everyone to roll the two dice. Whoever rolls the lowest total has to drink the ensuing cocktail.

If you're lucky, you might get a simple whisky and coke. If you're really unlucky, you could end up having to down a Schnapps and coconut milk, or a crème de menthe and grapefruit juice. Be sure to locate the Gents before you drink.

Dice Men

Halfway through an evening of heavy drinking, it's often the simplest games that work the best. Complicated rules aren't great for booze-addled minds. This drinking game – which requires no skill whatsoever, just pure luck – is about as simple as you can get. Each player takes turns throwing one die. Roll a one, and he has to drink a one-finger's-width of booze; roll a two, and it's two-finger's-width; and so on, all the way up to a maximum of six.

Beer Hunter

Hollywood actors Robert De Niro and Christopher Walken would win this one, hands down. After all, they played the real-bullets version in the 1978 Vietnam War film, The Deer Hunter. The rules are simple, and, fortunately, there's no chance of blowing your brains out like the prisoners of war in the film.

Everyone takes an identical can of beer from the fridge. Best man shakes one of the cans really excessively. Now, while no one is looking, he hides the shaken-up can amongst the other cans so that no one knows where it is. Each player then chooses a can, holds it right in front of their face and flips the ring pull. One unlucky stag covers his head with fizzy beer, while the others sit back and enjoy their drinks at leisure.

007

It's late in the evening. Everyone's a little tired after a long stag party. Perhaps it's time to settle down in front of the telly and watch a movie. What about an old James Bond flick? Perfect. Perfect, that is, if you want the drinking to continue unabated.

This game works well if you choose an old James Bond movie that no one has seen recently. The idea is to watch the film as you would normally, but to set yourself drinking tasks whenever a stock Bond routine takes place. Decide on the rules beforehand. Perhaps you all drink every time Bond kills a baddie, or every time he snogs a Bond girl, or whenever he says 'The name's Bond. James Bond'. It's up to you when and how much you drink. But everyone must drink.

Roxanne

Remember that 1980s rock band, The Police, featuring Sting on lead vocals? One of their early singles – Roxanne – has nothing to do with alcohol but is ideal if you need a quick drinking game to liven up the party.

Simply give all the stags a large drink, cue up the song on your music player and press play. Listen carefully to the lyrics of the song. Every time Sting sings the name 'Roxanne', you must all take a large swig of your drink. It's easy at the start of the song when Roxanne gets just the odd mention, but brutal toward the end of the song as Sting repeats her name over and over again.

Match the Match

The vast majority of stag parties feature sport on the telly at some point. It sort of goes with the territory. But what if it's a really dull game? How can you liven it up?

Here's one suggestion. Split the stag party into two teams, with best man as one team captain and the groom as the other. Each team then has to follow one of the teams (or sportsmen) competing on the telly. Before the match starts, decide on the forfeits. For example, if you're watching football, everyone on your team may have to drink every time your team takes a corner or a throw-in – double drinks if you concede a goal. If you're watching snooker, it might be one drink every time your player pots a coloured ball and double drinks if he pots the white.

Pub Golf

This is a pub crawl where you keep score. Hard-core drinkers can play 18 holes (in other words, 18 pubs visited), while mere mortals should stick to nine holes (nine pubs visited).

At each pub you visit, all the players must try to down their pints of beer in as few gulps as possible. Just like real golf, it's better to finish your drink with the fewest gulps possible. And just like golf, the overall winner is the drinker with the overall lowest score.

Off-Ground Groom

This is the perfect game for a large, rowdy stag party. And it's a surefire way of making yourselves very unpopular down the pub. The rules are as follows: Any time one of the stags shouts out the groom's name, everyone (groom included) must get off the floor as quickly and in any way possible. That might mean sitting on the bar, climbing onto a table, hanging from a chandelier and so on – just as long as no part of your body is touching the floor.

The last person to leave the floor has to down his drink.

Booze Relay

They never featured this sport at the Olympics, even though it requires a certain athleticism. Split the stag party into two teams with, as usual, best man captain of one team and the groom captain of the other. Place a whole load of opened cans of beer on the floor at the far end of the room. Stags now take turns in running from one end of the room to the other in search of a beer. The only catch is that they must do it blindfolded. Once they reach the beer, they must down a whole can and run back to their team where the next stag (also blindfolded) will then continue the relay. The losing team has to finish off any remaining beers.

Given the obvious carnage, this game is better played with cans rather than bottles of beer.

Card Sharp

It's a card game, but unlike any you've played before. Place a full pack of cards on top of a bottle of spirits. (It's up to the best man to choose what type of spirit, but, unless you want the party to end early, choose one that's not too strong.)

Players now take turns at blowing cards off the top of the deck. But beware: Should you blow too hard and knock the whole deck off, you have to drink a forfeit. The idea is to blow off just a few so that you pass your turn to the person next to you.

It's funny how your ability to blow gently diminishes with every forfeit you drink.

Appendix

Surfing the Best Man Web

• •

*T*hroughout this book, I've made suggestions as to what you can do as best man – from stag do ideas to a few gags for your speech. However, I can include only a limited number of ideas in the text of a book of this size, so this appendix points you in the right direction to explore the varied, wider world of the best man, listing the most useful websites for you to look at.

Wedding Basics

These websites fill in the blanks as to what everyone else does at the wedding, what the bride and bridesmaids go through in the buildup and other such crucial information.

- ✔ **Confetti** (www.confetti.co.uk). This website offers a wide-ranging guide to wedding fashion, venues, suppliers, honeymoons and guest lists.

- ✔ **Getting Married.co.uk** (www.gettingmarried.co.uk). This innovative website takes the headache out of the more tedious aspects of wedding planning such as invitations, gift lists, hotel booking, seating plans and online photo albums.

- ✔ **Hitched.co.uk** (www.hitched.co.uk). Very broad in its scope, this website offers advice for the best man (and other members of the wedding party), an online shop, ideas for wedding venues, an online wedding planner and discussion forums for all parties.

- ✔ **The National Wedding Show** (www.nationalwedding show.co.uk). Held in London and Birmingham, these wedding fairs offer plenty of ideas to all involved – mostly for brides and grooms, but it never hurt the best man to know a little more about what's going on around him.

✔ **Wedding Site** (www.weddingsite.co.uk). This website is great for planning the logistics of the wedding, sorting out the invitations and guest plans and keeping on top of the budget.

Hunting for the Stag Do

Chapters 2 and 3 go into plenty of detail about the all-important stag do, but if you're still stuck for ideas, I present a few more for you here, along with companies you can pay to do the thinking for you.

Stag do organisers

Bear in mind just how much work goes into organising a great stag do. Tickets, activities, evening venues and transport all need to be sorted, and the bulk of the organisation often needs to be done in a place you may never have visited before. Stag do organisers can take a lot of the load off your shoulders – for a fee.

The websites here range from organisers specialising in particular destinations or activities to good all-rounders who help you choose from a wide range of options.

✔ **The Barcelona Adventure Company:** www.barcelona adventure.com; 0871-711-5068

✔ **Bespoke Weekends:** www.bespokeweekends.co.uk; 0131 476 2474

✔ **Chillisauce:** www.chillisauce.co.uk; 020 7299 1831

✔ **Design Adventure:** www.designaventure.co.uk; 01432 830880

✔ **Eclipse Leisure:** www.eclipseleisure.co.uk; 01273 872230

✔ **Edinburgh Stag & Hen Weekends:** www.edinburgh stagandhen.co.uk; 0131 450 7113

✔ **Escape:** www.escapetrips.co.uk; 0117 9277173

✔ **Freedom:** www.freedomltd.com; 01992 655580

✔ **Garlands Off Road and Corporate Leisure:** www. garlandsleisure.co.uk; 01827-722123

✔ **Hen & Stag World:** www.henandstagworld.co.uk; 0191 206 4027

✔ **Ice Cube Party Weekends:** www.ice-cube.co.uk; 01943 872415

✔ **justplanetevents:** www.justplanetevents.com; 0845-222-3502

✔ **Last Night of Freedom:** www.lastnightoffreedom. co.uk; 0845 2602800

✔ **Maximise:** www.maximise.co.uk; 020 8236 0111

✔ **Mountain Mayhem:** www.mountainmayhem.com; 01873-860450

✔ **Party Bus:** www.partybus.co.uk; 0845-838-5400

✔ **Redseven Leisure:** www.redsevenleisure.co.uk; 0800 970 2744

✔ **Senor Stag:** www.senorstag.com; 01773 766052

✔ **The Stag Company:** www.thestagcompany.com; 01273 225 070

✔ **The Stag and Hen Company:** www.thestagandhen company.co.uk; 0844 804 5370

✔ **The Stag and Hen Experience:** www.thestagand henexperience.com; 01202 566100

✔ **Stag Party:** www.stagparty.co.uk; 01273 872230

✔ **Stagweb:** www.stagweb.co.uk; 0845-130-5225

✔ **Stag Weekends:** www.stagweekends.co.uk; 01773 766051

✔ **Superfun Stag Weekends:** www.superfunstag weekends.com

Stag do venues and events

If you're determined – and organised – enough to handle the stag do on your own, use this list to choose and arrange a day or weekend to suit the whole party.

✔ **Bungee jumping:** UK Bungee Club; www.ukbungee. co.uk; 07000 286433

✔ **Circus skills:** Circus Magic; http://uk.circusmagic. co.uk; 07920 400 309

✔ **Coasteering:** International Coasteering Association; www. coasteering.org; 0800 781 6861

✔ **Falconry:** Falconer's Retreat; www.falconersretreat. co.uk; 01984 634178

✔ **Ferrari driving:** Red Letter Days; www.redletterdays. co.uk; 0845 640 8000

✔ **Gliding:** British Gliding Association; www.gliding. co.uk; 0116 289 2956

✔ **Go-karting:** National Karting Association; www.national karting.co.uk; 01206-322726

✔ **Hot rod driving:** Red Letter Days; www.redletterdays. co.uk; 0845 640 8000

✔ **Ice cricket:** Tours 4 Sport; www.icecricket.co.uk; 01869 369765

✔ **Kite buggying:** Extreme Academy; www.watergatebay. co.uk; 01637-860543

✔ **Laser gun fighting:** Laser Mission; www.laser-mission. com; 0845 373 1838

✔ **MiG jet flying:** Red Letter Days; www.redletterdays. co.uk; 0845 640 8000

✔ **Military activities:** Chillisauce; www.chillisauce. co.uk; 020 7299 1831

✔ **Motor sports:** Trackdays; www.trackdays.co.uk; 01376 336701

✔ **Mountain boarding:** Another World Adventure Centre; www.mountainboarding.co.uk; 01422-245196

✔ **Mountaineering:** British Mountaineering Club; www. thebmc.co.uk; 0161 445 6111;

✔ **Paintballing:** UK Paintball Sports Federation; www. ukpsf.com; 0845-130-4252

✔ **Paragliding and hang gliding:** British Hang Gliding and Paragliding Association; www.bhpa.co.uk; 0116-289-4316

- ✔ **Quad biking:** Quad Racing Association UK; www.qrauk.com; 07774 434468

- ✔ **Running with bulls in Pamplona:** PP Travel; www.pptravel.com; 020 7930 9999

- ✔ **Scuba diving:** British Sub-Aqua Club; www.bsac.com; 0151-350-6200

- ✔ **Surfing:** Surfing Great Britain; http://surfinggb.com; 07967 664643

- ✔ **Tank driving:** Great Experience Days; www.greatexperiencedays.co.uk; 0870-199-3355.

- ✔ **Wakeboarding:** Wakeboard UK; www.wakeboard.co.uk

- ✔ **Windsurfing:** UK Windsurfing Association; www.ukwindsurfing.com

Stag do accessories

Gently embarrassing the stag is a key part of the celebrations. These websites help with kitting him out in the most suitable – or unsuitable – fashion.

- ✔ **Celebrations** (www.celebrations-party.co.uk). Everything from T-shirt printing to inflatable novelties.

- ✔ **Partybox** (www.partybox.co.uk). Wide range of party products from invitations through to wigs, masks and novelties.

- ✔ **Party Domain** (www.partydomain.co.uk). Wide range of party and fancy dress supplies.

- ✔ **Partyrama** (www.partyrama.co.uk). Costumes, balloons, fancy dress and the obligatory blow-up dolls.

- ✔ **Piggi Clothing** (www.piggi-clothing.co.uk). Specialist T-shirt designers and printers.

- ✔ **Silly Jokes** (www.sillyjokes.co.uk). Party pranks, accessories and costumes.

- ✔ **Stagnightout** (www.stagnightout.com). What to wear, what to do, games to play: lots of ideas for every stag do.

Online photo and video galleries

Keep a record of the stag do – you may need your memory jogging by posting the pictures or videos online.

Photo-sharing websites:

- ✔ www.flickr.com
- ✔ http://imageshack.us
- ✔ http://memeo.com
- ✔ http://beta.photobucket.com
- ✔ http://pinterest.com
- ✔ http://picasa.google.com
- ✔ www.photobox.co.uk

Video-sharing websites:

- ✔ http://YouTube.com
- ✔ http://Blip.tv
- ✔ http://Vimeo.com
- ✔ www.viddler.com
- ✔ www.dailymotion.com

Organising the Wedding Day

Not all best men are involved with the planning of the wedding day, but if you've rolled your sleeves up and are mucking in, the websites in this section are useful.

Limousine hire

Hiring a stretch limo (or a Hummer!) is a great idea for the stag do, even if you don't need to sort one out for the wedding day.

- ✔ **Cars for Stars** (www.carsforstars.net). From top-of-the-range Mercs to stretch limos.

  ✔ **England Limousines** (www.englandlimousines.
  co.uk). Chauffeur-driven Range Rovers, Mercs, Bentleys
  and Rollers.

  ✔ **Limo Broker** (www.limobroker.co.uk). Nationwide
  limousine hire specialising in stretch limos.

  ✔ **Limo Crazy** (www.limocrazy.co.uk). American stretch
  and standard limousines.

Get your kit on

Here are a few places that can help you get properly dressed
for the big day:

  ✔ **Anthony Formalwear:** Very modern and even a bit
  over the top, if that's what you're after (www.anthony
  formalwear.co.uk; 01277-651140).

  ✔ **Hugh Harris:** Based in Woking, Surrey, this company is
  small but very experienced. They stock some designer
  names, too (www.hughharris.co.uk; 01483 756267).

  ✔ **Moss Bros Hire:** The biggest company in the game, with
  over 130 stores nationwide. The prices are great value,
  too (www.moss.co.uk).

  ✔ **Neal & Palmer:** From Nehru jackets to frockcoats and
  morning suits, this Jermyn Street shop stocks 'em all
  (www.nealandpalmer.com; 020-7495-4094).

  ✔ **21st Century Kilts:** The Scots among you can try this
  Edinburgh-based hire shop (www.21stcenturykilts.
  com).

  ✔ **Young's Hire:** Dozens of concessions across the UK and
  Ireland (www.youngs-hire.co.uk).

  ✔ **Swarbrick's Formal Hire:** This Manchester-based outlet
  has a huge showroom and every type of wedding suit on
  offer (www.swarbricks.co.uk; 0161 643 4040).

Sorting Out Your Speech

Witty writing doesn't come easily to everyone, and we're not
all blessed with a memory for famous quotations. If that's true
of you, the websites in this section lend a helping hand.

Speech ideas

These websites offer a combination of speech advice and paid-for speech-writing services:

- ✔ http://artofmanliness.com. Nothing like a bit of old-fashioned, manly speech advice.
- ✔ www.thebestmanspeech.com. Comprehensive listing of material, examples and templates to help you plan your speech.
- ✔ www.a-best-man-speech.co.uk. Featuring custom-written speeches, inexpensive speech templates and a directory of humour.
- ✔ www.bestmanspeeches.com. Custom-written speeches for best men with little time or inclination to write their own speeches.
- ✔ www.hitched.co.uk. Speech advice and help as part of a general site for wedding ideas.
- ✔ www.the-asc.org.uk. The Association of Speakers' Clubs official website, offering advice on presentation and delivery of speeches.

Sources of quotations

A good quotation is a great way to bring a speech to its conclusion. The websites in this section help you out with quotes and poems to bring polish to your speech.

- ✔ www.lovepoemsandquotes.com. Verse and quotations to give your speech that extra sparkle.
- ✔ www.poemhunter.com. A UK website with plenty of wedding poems and quotations.
- ✔ www.poemsforfree.com. Over 1,500 free-to-use poems for every occasion – including best man speeches.
- ✔ www.weddinglovequotes.com. Slushy quotations guaranteed to get the bride and groom blushing.

Sources of jokes

You probably already have enough funny stuff about the groom, but these sites help with a few gags to get your audience in the mood.

- ✔ www.ahajokes.com. Hundreds of clean jokes organised by category.

- ✔ www.bestmanhelp.com. Classic jokes for a classic best man's speech.

- ✔ www.thebestmanspeech.com. Huge collection of speech jokes.

Index

• G •

• H •

• I •

About the Author

Dominic Bliss is former editor of the men's wedding magazine *Stag & Groom*. He has worked as a journalist since the early 1990s and currently works as a freelance writer for various men's interest and sports magazines. Married himself in the 2000s, he has attended more weddings than he can remember, starring as best man at a few of them.

Dedication

To Sally.

Author's Acknowledgments

A big thank-you to my wife, Sally. If you hadn't said 'I do', this book would never have been written. And to my brother, Jeremy, who was best man at my own wedding.

Publisher's Acknowledgments

We're proud of this book; please send us your comments at http://dummies.custhelp.com. For other comments, please contact our Customer Care Department within the U.S. at 877-762-2974, outside the U.S. at (001) 317-572-3993, or fax 317-572-4002.

Some of the people who helped bring this book to market include the following:

Acquisitions, Editorial, and Vertical Websites

Project Editor: Kelly Ewing
  (Previous Edition: Simon Bell)

Commissioning Editor: Mike Baker

Assistant Editor: Ben Kemble

Development Editor: Kelly Ewing

Copy Editor: Kelly Ewing

Production Manager: Dan Mersey

Publisher: Miles Kendall

Cover Photos: © Justin Horrocks / iStockphoto

Composition Services

Sr. Project Coordinator: Kristie Rees

Layout and Graphics: Melanee Habig

Proofreader: Jessica Kramer

Indexer: Potomac Indexing, LLC

For Dummies®

Making Everything Easier!™

UK editions

BUSINESS

978-1-118-34689-1

978-1-118-44349-1

978-1-119-97527-4

MUSIC

978-1-119-94276-4

978-0-470-97799-6

978-0-470-66372-1

HOBBIES

978-1-118-41156-8

978-1-119-99417-6

978-1-119-97250-1

Asperger's Syndrome For Dummies
978-0-470-66087-4

Basic Maths For Dummies
978-1-119-97452-9

Body Language For Dummies,
2nd Edition
978-1-119-95351-7

Boosting Self-Esteem For Dummies
978-0-470-74193-1

Business Continuity For Dummies
978-1-118-32683-1

Cricket For Dummies
978-0-470-03454-5

Diabetes For Dummies, 3rd Edition
978-0-470-97711-8

eBay For Dummies, 3rd Edition
978-1-119-94122-4

English Grammar For Dummies
978-0-470-05752-0

Flirting For Dummies
978-0-470-74259-4

IBS For Dummies
978-0-470-51737-6

ITIL For Dummies
978-1-119-95013-4

Management For Dummies,
2nd Edition
978-0-470-97769-9

Managing Anxiety with CBT
For Dummies
978-1-118-36606-6

Neuro-linguistic Programming
For Dummies, 2nd Edition
978-0-470-66543-5

Nutrition For Dummies, 2nd Edition
978-0-470-97276-2

Organic Gardening For Dummies
978-1-119-97706-3

FOR DUMMIES®

Making Everything Easier! ™

UK editions

SELF-HELP

Cognitive Behavioural Therapy

978-0-470-66541-1

Creative Visualization

978-1-119-99264-6

Mindfulness

978-0-470-66086-7

LANGUAGES

Spanish

978-0-470-68815-1

Polish

978-1-119-97959-3

British Sign Language

978-0-470-69477-0

HISTORY

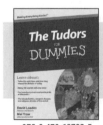

The Tudors

978-0-470-68792-5

Medieval History

978-0-470-74783-4

British History

978-0-470-97819-1

Origami Kit For Dummies
978-0-470-75857-1

Overcoming Depression For Dummies
978-0-470-69430-5

Positive Psychology For Dummies
978-0-470-72136-0

PRINCE2 For Dummies, 2009 Edition
978-0-470-71025-8

Project Management For Dummies
978-0-470-71119-4

Psychology Statistics For Dummies
978-1-119-95287-9

Psychometric Tests For Dummies
978-0-470-75366-8

Renting Out Your Property For
Dummies, 3rd Edition
978-1-119-97640-0

Rugby Union For Dummies, 3rd Edition
978-1-119-99092-5

Sage One For Dummies
978-1-119-95236-7

Self-Hypnosis For Dummies
978-0-470-66073-7

Storing and Preserving Garden
Produce For Dummies
978-1-119-95156-8

Teaching English as a Foreign
Language For Dummies
978-0-470-74576-2

Time Management For Dummies
978-0-470-77765-7

Training Your Brain For Dummies
978-0-470-97449-0

Voice and Speaking Skills For Dummies
978-1-119-94512-3

Work-Life Balance For Dummies
978-0-470-71380-8

DUMMIES®

Making Everything Easier! ™

COMPUTER BASICS

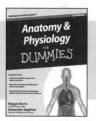

978-1-118-11533-6

978-0-470-61454-9

978-0-470-49743-2

DIGITAL PHOTOGRAPHY

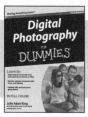

978-1-118-09203-3

978-0-470-76878-5

978-1-118-00472-2

SCIENCE AND MATHS

978-0-470-92326-9

978-0-470-55964-2

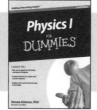

978-0-470-90324-7

Art For Dummies
978-0-7645-5104-8

Computers For Seniors For Dummies, 3rd Edition
978-1-118-11553-4

Criminology For Dummies
978-0-470-39696-4

Currency Trading For Dummies, 2nd Edition
978-0-470-01851-4

Drawing For Dummies, 2nd Edition
978-0-470-61842-4

Forensics For Dummies
978-0-7645-5580-0

French For Dummies, 2nd Edition
978-1-118-00464-7

Guitar For Dummies, 2nd Edition
978-0-7645-9904-0

Hinduism For Dummies
978-0-470-87858-3

Index Investing For Dummies
978-0-470-29406-2

Islamic Finance For Dummies
978-0-470-43069-9

Knitting For Dummies, 2nd Edition
978-0-470-28747-7

Music Theory For Dummies, 2nd Edition
978-1-118-09550-8

Office 2010 For Dummies
978-0-470-48998-7

Piano For Dummies, 2nd Edition
978-0-470-49644-2

Photoshop CS6 For Dummies
978-1-118-17457-9

Schizophrenia For Dummies
978-0-470-25927-6

WordPress For Dummies, 5th Edition
978-1-118-38318-6

Think you can't learn it in a day? Think again!

The *In a Day* e-book series from *For Dummies* gives you quick and easy access to learn a new skill, brush up on a hobby, or enhance your personal or professional life — all in a day. Easy!